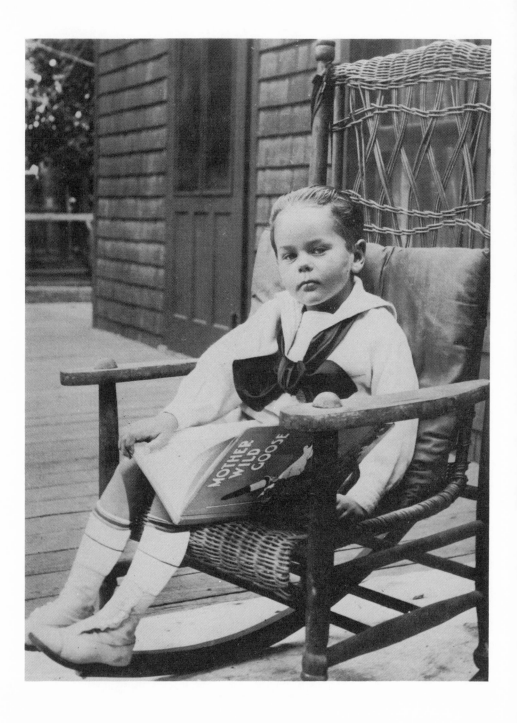

James Broughton Coming Unbuttoned

A Memoir

CITY LIGHTS

SAN FRANCISCO

COMING UNBUTTONED

Cover photograph by Marc Geller
Cover design by John Miller, Big Fish Books
Book design by Nancy J. Peters

Library of Congress Cataloging-in-Publication-Data

Broughton, James Richard, 1913-
    Coming unbuttoned : a memoir / by James Broughton.
        p.   cm.
    ISBN 0-87286-280-1 : $9.95
    1. Broughton, James Richard, 1913-   — Biography.   2. Poets,
American — 20th century — Biography.   3. Motion picture producers and
directors — United States — Biography.   I. Title.
PS3503.R759Z464   1993
811'.54 — dc20
    [B]   93-24489
                                                                    CIP

City Lights Books are available to bookstores through our primary distributor:
Subterranean Company, P. O. Box 160, 265 S. 5th St., Monroe, OR 97456.
503-847-5274. Toll-free orders 800-274-7826. FAX 503-847-6018. Our books
are also available through library jobbers and regional distributors. For personal
orders and catalogs, please write to City Lights Books, 261 Columbus Avenue,
San Francisco, CA 94133.

CITY LIGHTS BOOKS are edited by Lawrence Ferlinghetti and Nancy J. Peters
and published at the City Lights Bookstore, 261 Columbus Avenue,
San Francisco, CA 94133.

To James Leo Herlihy
my ideal reader

I owe thanks for this book to
Mark Zadrozny who initiated it,
Mark Thompson who insisted on it,
Lawrence Ferlinghetti who commissioned it,
Nancy J. Peters who chaperoned it,
Joel Singer who nourished it,
Alex Gildzen who embellished it,
and to Lynn Nowak who dragged it out of me.

A NOTE FROM THE AUTHOR

I have not included in this book everything I think I know nor everyone I may have met. I have not tried to be polite or fair or thorough. I have recorded only what amused me to recall.

Memory may forget a lot but it never forgets what should have occurred. All the events in this book are true, including those that did not happen.

If a reader finds this chronicle uneven, unclear, or unbelievable I would reply that such was my experience of life.

CONTENTS

1

INTO THIS WORLD AND OUT OF IT

THE YEAR that gave birth to *Le Sacre du Printemps, Swann's Way,* and *Nude Descending a Staircase* also brought me into this world. Those other blessed events of 1913 required a more laborious parturition than I did. Dr. Robertson declared mine the happiest delivery he had ever attended. For one thing I sailed in easy and laughing. And because I smiled at everyone they called me Sunny Jim. This happened in the town of Modesto on the Tuolomne River of Stanislaus County in the state of California.

My mother once confessed that giving birth to me was the orgasmic highlight of her life. In fact, she and I got along better in her womb than we ever did after I came out of it. She adored babies but disliked children, disliked indeed any person who ignored her instructions. Once I crawled around on my own she found plenty to dislike.

My initial misdemeanor remained the most unforgivable. No firstborn son of hers had any right turning out to be a poet. She had planned it: I was to be a surgeon, marry a girl from a good family, play golf with Republicans, and earn uncountable sums of money. After all, my grandfathers were bankers, and so was my father. Poets didn't know how to earn money and didn't care to know. They led disreputable lives and died young. Besides, most of them were sissies and everyone knew that sissies wouldn't defend themselves, wouldn't even fight for their country. They went on the stage or got arrested for indecent behavior. If Sunny Jim showed such tendencies she would have to squelch them at once. Thus, although I was born cheerful, my mother did her utmost to beat the cheer out of me.

Named Olga Matilda Jungbluth, my mother held stern Prussian notions of how a man should act. Her grandfather embodied this ideal of manhood. Nicholas Ohlandt had arrived from Germany with only seven dollars in his pocket (so went the family legend) and when he departed for Cypress Lawn Cemetery he was president of the San Francisco Bank where he made money and president of the National Ice Company where he made ice cream. Olga was his favorite in the family and she adored him in return. She named my baby brother Nicholas in the hope that he would grow into a great tycoon. Though he was not a sissy, he too proved to be an economic disappointment.

Olga had little patience with my father's diffidence toward moneymaking. She also deplored his small-town heritage. Orphaned as a child, she had been raised in a lap of luxury by the Ohlandts in their Queen Anne mansion on a San Francisco hilltop. To have ended her honeymoon in a dinky bungalow in a flat farming town of the San Joaquin Valley was both an indignity and a tribulation. In this bungalow — 1015 16th Street, Modesto, California — Dr. Robertson introduced me to planet Earth when the sun was in Scorpio, the moon in Aires, and Libra rising. My mother was a double Virgo.

Three years later in this same bungalow I experienced the major epiphany of my life. In a book and a film I have described the experience thus: "One night when I was three years old I was awakened by a glittering stranger who told me I was a poet and always would be and never to fear being alone or being laughed at. That was my first meeting with my angel, who is the most interesting poet I have ever met."

The actual event was not so concisely perceived. Being so much a part of everything he sees, a wide-eyed child is an imprecise reporter. Nor does my statement of the fact mean that anyone has believed it. In 1942 a psychiatrist in West Los Angeles scoffed at me: "That shows how weak your sense of reality has always been." William Blake would have believed me. But then Blake never went to a therapist. He knew that poets never lie, they merely embroider.

It must have happened on an autumn night of 1916 before my brother was born. I remember waking in the dark and hearing my parents arguing in the next room. But a more persistent sound, a kind of whirring whistle, spun a light across the ceiling. I stood up in my crib and looked into the backyard. Over the neighbor's palm tree a pulsing headlamp came whistling directly toward me. When it had whirled right up to my window, out of its radiance stepped a naked boy. He was at least three years older than I but he looked all ages at once. He had no wings, but I knew he was angel-sent: his laughing beauty illuminated the night and his melodious voice enraptured my ears.

I didn't know what his words meant but I understood everything he said. And he said a lot. He said I could call him Hermy though that was not his real name. He knew my name because it was on his agenda. He represented a company whose business was health care for the soul. And he wanted me to work for them.

He insisted I would always be a poet even if I tried not to be. He offered me three gifts that he said would come in handy: intuition, articulation, and merriment. Poets, he explained, believe in the unbelievable, worship wonder, celebrate life. Despite what I might hear to the contrary the world was not a miserable prison, it was a playground for a nonstop tournament between stupidity and imagination. If I followed the game sharply enough I could be a useful spokesman for Big Joy. I know this is what he said because he told me the same sort of thing at many a later meeting.

As he spoke he drew forth from the glow between his legs a pulsing hot sparkler which laughed the way he did. Raising it like a wand he circled my head with stars, then spilled them on my brow, my throat, my chest, all the way down to my peepee. The hot sparks made me giggle.

When he blessed me that way I knew I would always belong to him. (I realize now that he neglected to bless my feet. Perhaps angels don't think much about feet. This may account for my difficulty in standing my ground as well as my tendency to collapse upwards.)

Suddenly Hermy blew out his throbbing wand, spun back into his searchlight and zoomed out of sight over the palm tree just as I heard my mother enter from her bedroom: "Good Lord, baby! Why are you standing up? Are you sick? Heavens, you've wet your jammies again!"

I never told my mother about my secret visitor. She had short patience with extraterrestrial mysteries. Marrying into an Episcopalian family had only increased her irritation with the inexplicable. Moral prejudices were sufficient for her. When it came to dealing with sin she venerated surgeons because they could cut the bad out of one. I had to keep many secrets from her for fear she would have me operated on regularly. All my life Hermy remained my biggest secret.

I would like to have told my father. He seemed pleased that I was growing up. But I had too little chance to share his company. He died two years later.

At an art auction in 1959 a hostess pouring me a cup of tea remarked: "Your father was the handsomest man I ever met in my entire life." She had been his classmate at Berkeley in 1904. "Irwin Broughton was a real knockout," she added. On the other hand my mother, who never attended university, had this to say: "Your father drove me crazy. I never had any idea what he was thinking."

For me he was never less than a godlike figure with his warm bulk, his arms that lifted me aloft, his resonant voice. I especially remember rides with him: riding on his shoulders at a Fourth of July parade, riding in the saddle with him on one of Bob McHenry's palominos at the Bald Eagle Ranch, riding down a slide in a wooden boat at an amusement park. He never made fun of me. He didn't seem to worry that I preferred Raggedy Andy to a baseball bat. My behavior amused more than annoyed him. Like the occasion in the Santa Cruz mountains during the last summer of his life when, dressed up for dinner at the resort hotel, I fell into Boulder Creek. I had leaned too far over the water reaching for a frog. When Irwin pulled me out dripping and crying he consoled me warmly whereas Olga berated me for ruining my brand-new sailor suit.

The most disturbing memory I have of my father happened the night Olga ordered him to punish me. After my brother's birth we had moved from Modesto to a house on Clay Street in San Francisco near my mother's relatives. My father worked in the Federal Reserve. One day, after slapping me several times, Olga fumed, "I'm tired of trying to discipline you. When your father comes home I'll get him to give you a good beating. Maybe he can teach you not to be so naughty."

When I heard Irwin enter the house I hid in the hall closet behind the carpet sweeper. Olga told him that I had gone the limit this time: "Do you know what that little devil did? He put on my new feathered turban and then emptied a bottle of Milk of Magnesia over Baby Nick. The rug is ruined."

I squinched as far into the corner as I could. When he pulled me out I felt more fearful than guilty. Whereas Olga frequently swatted me as though I were a bothersome fly, Irwin had never raised his hand to me. Now pushing me along the back hall he announced, "I'm taking you down to the basement, young man, to teach you a lesson."

We descended the steep stairs into the cellar which housed the furnace and the water heater and the lawn mower. But once there Irwin stopped and stood still. He didn't start to whip me, he seemed to forget all about me. When he did recollect why we were there, he sighed, "You shouldn't upset your mother so much, she's high-strung."

Gently he took me by the hand and sat me down beside him on the bottom stair. Then he put his arm around my shoulder and drew me close to him. For the longest time he held me in his arms, emitting occasional gasps and weary sighs. He stared into the dark as he spoke:

"Do you remember Justin? My friend Justin? When he was last here we took you to Idora Park, do you remember, and we rode on the Chute-the-Chutes?"

I not only remembered how the boat slid down into a splashing lake, I remembered sitting between my father and a red-bearded fellow who shouted "Ship Ahoy!" Never before had I seen my father so boisterous. But here in the cold basement his body slumped heavily upon me as he murmured, "He's gone. Justin's gone — he's gone for good." And he began to cry.

Years later I learned that on the very day of his not spanking me Irwin had received news of his friend's death in a French hospital. Justin had been fatally wounded in the Battle of the Marne.

When I was in my teens my father's sister told me how much Justin meant to Irwin, how they had been close chums in college, had trekked in the Rockies and fished in the Gulf, partnered in land schemes in Oregon, were in fact inseparable. But when Justin proposed that they set forth on a greater adventure — working their way around the world on freighters — the camaraderie hit a snag. Justin had no family ties but Irwin's parents had been pressuring him to settle down and take his place in his father's bank. The choice was further complicated by Irwin's infatuation with a San Francisco debutante to whom he had proposed. Separation from Justin was painful. Vivid letters from exotic ports increased the pain. Justin even wrote a book called *From Job to Job Around the World* which I discovered one summer in my grandfather's bookcase, well-thumbed and fondly inscribed to my father.

For his last call to adventure Justin had proposed that he and Irwin enlist together in the AEF, go to France and show those Huns where to get off. This outraged Olga. Not only did Irwin have ample exemptions with job and family, but she was not about to tolerate his deserting her to go shooting Germans.

The day after learning of Justin's death Irwin, without informing Olga, enlisted in the army and requested duty in the machine-gun corps. Before he could be called up, the Armistice was signed (on the day after my fifth birthday). Irwin took the Armistice as a personal frustration and several times came home rowdy drunk. Then I came home from kindergarten with the influenza virus.

The epidemic victimized everyone in the household except the German cook. Pneumonia complicated my mother's condition. My baby brother barely survived. It was my husky handsome father who perished. Since I was the first to recover I was the last member of the family to see him alive. In defiance of doctor's orders and nurse's protests he had dragged himself from his sickbed, determined to go downtown to his office. Passing the bathroom I saw him at the basin honing his razor. He smiled weakly and sighed and urged me to do things like stay well and be good and grow up big. I ran forward and grabbed his leg and held on until he bent down and gave me a kiss that left lather on my cheek. I didn't wipe it off.

He was brought home in an ambulance and died in the night without regaining consciousness.

Though my mother excelled in finding fault, with my father's family I enjoyed total approval. I was named James Richard after my paternal grandfather who displayed me proudly at the Modesto Elks and Rotary club luncheons as his "Number One Grandson." He took pride in his whole family tree. He told me that his father, Job Broughton, had been a scout with Fremont before the Gold Rush and that his mother, Celia Irwin, had come from St. Jo, Missouri, in a covered wagon. In the early eighteenth century English-born Broughtons had emigrated from Somerset to the

Carolinas. Later ancestors included a captain in Washington's army and a cousin who gave birth to Daniel Boone.

Grandfather worked his way up from janitor to president of the Modesto Bank. He signed himself J. R. Broughton, even in letters to close relatives. He stood ramrod erect, his white beard tawny from cigar smoke. He wore three-piece suits and black ties that would have looked correct on Abraham Lincoln. He kept chickens in the backyard, loved to play pinochle, tell jokes on women, and brag about his youth as a vaquero in the Almaden of San Jose. I lived in devoted awe of him: he possessed unshakable integrity, a twinkling eye, and the fragrance of a live oak in midsummer.

There was another "Sunny Jim" in the family, my father's uncle, Jim Hammond, a spry eighty-year-old bachelor with a silky white mustache. He tickled and cuddled me whenever I had the luck to visit him. He lived in the abandoned Mother Lode town of La Grange on the upper Tuolomne where he and my grandmother's brother, George Bates, had opened a general store in the heyday of gold mining. By the early 1920s Hammond & Bates was a musty place still crammed with gold-digging equipment, yardage, arrow-heads, coal oil lamps, corsets, and a miscellany of antiquated oddities in undusted cases. At that late date Mr. Hammond and Mr. Bates spent most of their time sitting on the front porch waiting for something to happen. Inside the store George's wife, Aunt Gussie, ran the infrequent business of the post office and the telephone exchange alongside her cash register.

Across the road in the parlor of the house where the three old folks lived wiry Uncle Jim rocked me on his lap while he regaled me with tales of his childhood trek to California: Indian raids, buffalo herds, flooding rivers, the death of a beloved brother in the Nevada desert. He would tap time against my tummy while he sang "Oh! Susanna!" in his soft lilting tenor, until Aunt Gussie came in with lemonade. On his eighty-first birthday she said, "Well, I guess Jim'll never get married now." When his will was probated in 1924 his bequest to me amounted to $17.31. Though I valued it as a precious legacy of my James lineage, my mother snatched the check away with a sneer and never gave me the money.

My father's mother, Jennie Bates, grew up in the town of Sonora when it was a booming center of the Mother Lode. When I knew her as Grandma Broughton in Modesto she was a stout, faded beauty fond of quoting Elbert Hubbard, embroidering samplers, and entertaining the Episcopal bishop. Her British ancestors from Springfield in Essex had been founders of Springfield, Massachusetts, in the seventeenth century, later moving west to establish Springfield, Illinois. From there her parents had come to California in quest of gold. Jennie's mother, however, could not stand the rough tedium of mining life: she ran off to Chicago with a dude gambler. Jennie never forgave her. All her life Jennie spoke righteously on the subject of loose women, convinced that sex led inevitably to disaster. One summer Saturday when I asked if I could go to the matinee of a movie with Ronald Colman and Vilma Banky called *One Night of Love*, she replied with a shudder, "Absolutely not!"

She never recovered from Irwin's sudden death at age thirty-five. He was the one and only darling of her heart. For the remainder of her life Jennie kept a fresh rose in front of his photograph on the mantel and almost always wore the lavender of Lent. She blamed the tragedy on my mother because Olga had taken him away from Modesto.

I was always pleased to be shipped off to Modesto for vacations. I loved my grandmother Jennie unreservedly, not only for her generosity with pancakes, butterscotch, and watermelon but because she indulged my appetite for dressing up, declaiming verse, practicing the hula, stringing beads, cutting out paper dolls, all the amusements that offended my mother. She let me dance to the Edison phonograph with nothing on but a scarf or two. I longed to be a dancer, a great dancer. For me dance was the most exultant form of poetry. If I couldn't dance — if I lost my legs, for instance — I vowed to be a dramatic poet, for I loved the magic of words and everything about the theater.

Jennie's house contained framed verses, embroidered homilies, and poetry volumes in soft leather bindings. There I first read Longfellow, Whittier, and Omar Khayyam. The first poem I ever memorized hung on the wall beside my brass bed in that house. Grinning goblins illustrated the text:

> There is so much good in the worst of us
> And so much bad in the best of us
> That it hardly behooves any of us
> To talk about the rest of us.

Other words of wisdom I have learned from frequent viewing of the printed broadside I acquired when I was sixty from the Tantric Buddhist of Berkeley, Rimpoche Tartang Tulku. This Tibetan verse perches above my toilet where one has to read it whenever one stands to urinate:

> Since everything is but an apparition
> perfect in being what it is,
> having nothing to do with good or bad,
> acceptance or rejection,
> one may well burst out in laughter.

This is credited to *The Natural Freedom of Mind* by Longchenpa, a fourteenth-century Tibetan poet.

Aside from forcing us to sing "O Tannenbaum" and "Stille Nacht" on Christmas Eve the only verse I associate with my mother is "This Little Pig Went to Market." Once in a while at my baby bedtime she would chant this rhyme as she tweaked my toes one by one until she reached "This little pig went squeak squeak squeak all the way home." I wondered if my toes were the only thing she liked about me. Olga had a fixation on feet. Maybe because both of her middle toes were abnormally long.

Did any of this influence the poem I wrote years later?

Papa has a pig.
And a big pig too.
Papa plays a piggy-toe that I can't do.
O papa has the biggest pig you ever did see.
He gave only ten little piggies to me.
    Papa has the star of all the swine,
    Papa shines stern in the sty. &c.

This actually was written about my stepfather, who was the biggest pig I knew as a child. I also wrote one about my mother, which begins:

What a big nose Mrs. Mother has,
the better to smell her dear.
Sniff sniff sniff it comes round the door,
detective of anything queer . . .

She was always checking us for boy crimes and misdemeanors, checking whether we had moved our bowels or said our prayers or parked chewing gum under the table. My own secret prayer began:

Now I lay me down to sleep,
I pray the Lord to help me out.
I'm flat on my back and left alone.
So God bless nobody, please keep out . . .

Unlike my grandmother Jennie, who sent me a missal and a hymnal bound in soft leather when I was confirmed at St. Paul's in San Rafael, my mother never showed any interest in my spiritual development. In Olga's family the prime usefulness of the Almighty, if invoked seriously, was to help one make money.

The Ohlandt mansion on Steiner Street contained four parlors and two dining rooms, an entrance hall large enough for weddings, and a third floor ballroom reached by an elevator. Nowadays it serves as a home for alcoholic Episcopalians. There is irony in this. Henry, the only son in the family, never did anything in his life but get drunk and concoct practical jokes, until he perished painfully of acute alcoholism. His three sisters — Tillie, Tootsie, and Freda — were addicted to jewelry and social climbing.

Their mother, my widowed great-grandmother Ohlandt, used to arrive corseted and veiled in her Locomobile towncar with a fancy basket full of stale bread to take my brother and me to Golden Gate Park to feed the ducks. I was awed by her thick German accent, her Queen Maryish toques and her extraordinary vehicle: a dark enclosed cab with roses in a cut glass vase, soft lap robes and gray silk window shades. The chauffeur out in front could be directed by way of a tube one shouted into. Alas, by 1920 the Locomobile and the mansion had to be sold. The old lady too lay dead.

In that year my mother moved us to a flat on Pacific Avenue across the street from Ulysses S. Grant Grammar School. Its attic playroom was spacious enough for all our games and quarrels. There I set up my toy theater, my Oz books, and my stage for theatricals. With congenial schoolmates I reenacted my versions of everything I saw on Saturday afternoon at the Orpheum vaudeville or on Sunday afternoon at the silent movies. My Aunt Marion, the childless wife of my alcoholic great-uncle, provided these regular treats. A fun-loving extrovert from Indianapolis, she also took us on motor trips to mountains and beaches. My mother never even took us to Golden Gate Park.

My father's sister, my Aunt Esto, was the only person who read poetry to me when I was a child. She brought me my first Mother Goose collection, as well as Eugene Field and *A Child's Garden of Verses* with the Jessie Wilcox Smith illustrations. How I wished Mother Goose had been my parent, she had such a frisky mind. Aunt Esto must have recognized that I was a social anomaly like herself, since she too was looked upon as an embarrassment to the family: she was dwarfed, walked with a limp, and was unmarried. But she had defied the small-town frumps, obtained a law degree from UC Berkeley, gone into politics and become one of the first women elected to the state Legislature.

Aunt Esto also had a passion for the theater. After careers in law and journalism, she joined the staff of the Pasadena Playhouse in its heyday, where I first saw *Julius Caesar*. When I was seven years old she had taken me and my little brother to a matinee of *The Merchant of Venice* with David Warfield playing Shylock. This elaborate Belasco production included a real ship for Antonio in the first scene, splashing fountains for Portia's garden at the end, and a lavish Venetian carnival in the middle. Such was my awakening to the enchantments of Shakespeare. My first literary guru, he taught me to think poetically, to keep imagination articulate, and to relish human diversity. At that *Merchant* matinee in the midst of the long moonlight scene of the lovers in the last act ("On such a night . . . ") my little brother piped up: "When's that old Jew coming back?" to the considerable disruption of the audience around us.

One winter in the late thirties when I was stranded temporarily in Bermuda I borrowed from the library in Hamilton the Oxford edition of the *Complete Works of W.S.* and prowled through the entire 1,352 pages of double-column small print, beginning with *The Tempest*. Though I had studied many of the plays in college I reveled anew in the agonies of kings and the innocence of lovers in song, soliloquy, and the ravishments of language. Any poet not enraptured by language might as well write obituary notices.

The Tempest has always been my favorite of the plays, probably because it is the one most obviously about a poet's magic. It is also the only one of the plays in which I have performed. Even that comprised but a single scene from the play, presented as a term project at the Hitchcock Military Academy in San Rafael, California, in 1924. In such a macho environment it was probably not surprising that I should have been the cadet selected to play Ariel.

In the scene chosen I was supposed to be invisible to Trinculo and Stephano during their drunken buffoonery. The only words I had to say, several times, were two: "Thou liest." But I was so panicked by stage fright that I peed in the wings, leaving a puddle to puzzle the stage manager. Years later at Stratford-on-Avon, in the summer of 1951, I watched Alan Badel perform Ariel to the Prospero of Michael Redgrave. Silver naked, slender as a magic wand, he was gracefully powerful enough to carry out any astonishment a poet might require.

To act out my passion for Shakespeare I took it upon myself to memorize Hamlet's soliloquy, "Oh, what a rogue and peasant slave am I!" while crossing the Pacific in the summer of 1934 on the S.S. *General Pershing*. My stepfather had passed on to me a round-trip ticket to Manila on this passenger-carrying cargo ship owned by a business friend of his. At the ship's concert on the night before we reached Hong Kong, I recited with the temerity of a twenty-year-old the entire speech more or less accurately. "What's Hecuba to him, or he to Hecuba, that he should weep for her?" Unfortunately a monsoon was descending upon us, and I was barely able to stand upright while members of the audience crept away to be sick in their cabins.

2

DORMITORY INITIATIONS

HOW DID I happen to be acting Ariel in a military academy when I was ten years old? This was due entirely to my mother's desperate widowhood. After my father's death she launched a relentless campaign to find a rich second husband.

She said, "I'll never again let a man pull the wool over my eyes. Your father left me nothing but debts. Money would disappear and I never knew what he did with it. I was so green, I was taken in by his good looks. He could charm the pants off a snake."

Dressing us in expensive clothes she took us to expensive resorts winter and summer — Tahoe, Del Monte, Coronado — where she flirted as fashionably as her desperation allowed. To make me more presentable she gummed my head with a glue called Bandoline. This was supposed to make my hair lie flat in a pompadour like the Kaiser's, whereas it preferred to fall forward in bangs.

I resented being made to smile at prospective stepfathers. I had forever lost the chance to laugh enough with my real father. Not surprisingly I moped more than I smiled. Sometimes I couldn't restrain my tears. This annoyed my mother: "What a namby-pamby sissy. One look at you and you start boohooing. You're just too sensitive for this world. If you don't quit this sulking I'll give you something to really cry about."

Any self-respecting poet would have felt too sensitive for my mother's world. Convinced that I was a liability in the eyes of any he-man suitor, Olga would introduce me as some pitiable mistake of nature. She never understood that sissies like poets are tougher than they look, that they learn early to sidestep and outwit and endure, that they giggle rather than growl because, being pariahs, they are free to laugh at the delusions of the world and to kiss the joys as they fly.

Despite the handicap of two small sons Olga had marriageable assets. She was a lithe dancer, a lucky gambler, a stylish dresser. She also possessed a hearty laugh though she didn't find much that was funny. Like the rest of her German clan she could switch in a twinkling from sentimental sobs to toilet jokes. One of her habitual sighings was, "I've been so busy all day I haven't had time to fart." Her days comprised a heavy schedule of gossiping, shopping, and mah jonging.

Very few of her husband candidates did I like. Scott Hendricks had huge black eyebrows and two huge dogs but was stingy. Wendell MacPherson smelled of horses, had a big nose, and owned a yacht. I liked the way he wrestled me but Olga thought him frivolous. The handsomest was Elliott Flugelhoff but she couldn't countenance being a Mrs. Flugelhoff. She scoffed when I asked her why she didn't marry Borge Nilsen. He was the husky blond ranger in Yosemite who at Christmastime had taken us cross-country skiing from the Sentinel Hotel. I worshipped his rugged warmth. I can never forget the toboggan ride he took me on one icy morning. He lay completely and snugly on top of me till I felt I was part of him, and off we sped down the steep slope at such exciting speed that when we reached the bottom I wet my pants. Maybe it was my first orgasm.

In the end Olga picked a man neither handsome, sophisticated, nor fun-loving. A self-made lumber baron from Hoquiam, Washington, Will Wood was not only rich, he was determined to get richer. Of my mother he often said, "I adore the ground she walks on." For years he would spoil my appetite at the dinner table by repeating, "Your mother is the most wonderful woman God ever made." As if that were not enough he would sometimes serenade her right in the middle of the roast beef with a loud outburst from *The Desert Song*: "One alone, to be my own, the one my worshipping soul possesses . . ." She would grin appropriately and not even look embarrassed.

Will had disliked me on first sight and the more he witnessed of my talents the more disgusted his dislike became. He especially disapproved of my theatricals and my theatrical behavior. In the attic playroom I had set up a rickety stage with some discarded drapes for curtains. There I often forced my baseball-loving brother to portray villains or servants. Sometimes for my leading lady I had to make do with cross-eyed Jane Newhall from across the street. I much preferred sultry black-haired Gloria Zander whose mother told fortunes in a storefront on Fillmore Street wearing gypsy costume. Gloria was my favorite playmate: she shared with me the movie magazines that she stole from the drugstore.

One day when Olga came home from a bridge party earlier than expected Gloria and I were in her bedroom playing dress-up. I had donned a beaded chiffon evening dress and a lamé cloche. In silver high heels I was sashaying about with a fan of pink ostrich feathers. To Gloria I had given a smaller purple fan that matched a velvet opera cloak. I had already decorated her with Olga's pearls. Hearing the front door slam and Olga's voice calling out I panicked. Hastily stashing the fans in their drawer I stumbled on the high heels and fell to my knees tearing the dress, as my mother entered the room.

"What's going on here?" Her familiar fury became cyclonic. Seeing Gloria, whom she loathed, she cried, "My God — my pearls!"

Removing them quickly and flinging off the cape, Gloria fled from the house. Then Olga said, "Now you, Jimmy Broughton — take off my dress!" The fact that I was naked underneath it only outraged her the more. She reached for her riding crop and beat me unmercifully.

That evening when Will Wood came to call she told him the whole story. He denounced me as the worst sissy he had ever heard of in his entire life and announced that he could not tolerate the prospect of living in the same house with a creature like me. Therefore I must go or he would. He said, "The next thing you know that boy will be sitting down to pee."

She and Will held a solemn conference. They agreed that making a man of me required stern measures. It was Will who proposed the military as a cure for my perversity. It was he who located the academy in San Rafael. It was his chauffeur who drove me over to the school with my suitcase of uniforms and name-labeled underwear. It was he, I suppose, who paid the tuition. Feeling well rid of me he married my mother before the year was out while I vowed that no one anywhere would make me into a man anything like him.

The dormitory for the youngest boys was a two-story barn with all the doors opening onto a central hall. I could not believe the bleakness of the narrow cell I was expected to occupy: bare wooden walls, bare floor, bare bulb from the ceiling, bare cot, uncurtained window looking out on the railroad track of the Northwestern Pacific. I felt I had been condemned to prison, under sentence of death.

When I heard someone in the hall approaching my door I ducked into the narrow closet, pulled its door shut, and crouched there until it grew dark and a bugle blew and footsteps came and went and the door to my room opened and I squeezed farther into the corner of the dark closet and then the door closed and everyone went away and I realized they must have gone to dinner and this way I would get nothing to eat, I would starve and be found dead here in the morning and no one would care, and it would serve my mother right. And I threw up in the closet.

How did I survive that barracky place that smelled of varnish and disinfectant and the urine of boys? I had never had to sweep my room or make my bed or polish a brass doorknob or load a rifle or carry it on my shoulder. I had never had to stand at rigid attention, pull in my butt, suck in my gut, and wear a heavy khaki uniform and puttees. Nor had I ever gone for cross-country runs at daybreak, been regulated by buglers, or eaten tasteless overcooked food. The most energetic game we had played on Pacific Avenue was Kick the Can.

At home I had been surrounded by women, scolded by women, taught by women, and been the playmate of girls. At the military school I was surrounded by male bodies, male smells, tough talk, rough games, sharp commands, tests of strength, dirty jokes, and dirty tricks. Inevitably I was made fun of. But so was everybody else. We were all misfits whose parents didn't know what to do with us. As fellow exiles we found congeniality. We even found affection.

My miserable cell had a magic peephole in the wall above my cot. It looked into the adjoining room where the house officer was billeted. I could hear Sergeant Naylor coming in after my lights were out, could hear him breathing after he got into bed. One night when I put my eye to that peephole my curiosity gasped. Where he stood naked leaning against his bed, Naylor's bare strong thighs and his amply developed genitals directly faced me. Apparently he was looking at a magazine by his overhead light bulb. I had never had an opportunity to observe any man's privates that closely. As the fingers of his right hand began to stroke his penis I saw it rouse and rise as he caressed it. Awed by the vision of a man enjoying his sexuality I went about for days in wonder. Could I do that with mine? Did all men inside their underpants sport shape-changing and explosive pendants? Even Jesus, under his diapers?

The anguish of my first weeks of school devastated my digestive system. Whatever I could not stomach, I threw up. So I was throwing up all over that military academy. No more than two months after school began I was hospitalized in San Francisco with acute appendicitis. The operation took place two days before my tenth birthday. The surgeon told me he had difficulty removing my appendix because, he said, "it had enlarged to bulging." He said it was the largest from anyone my age in the history of the hospital. He gave it to me in a bottle to take home.

All too soon I had to return to San Rafael. To impress the other boys I brought my appendix with me. One morning before reveille a pug-faced redhead named Clark Pettit slipped into my bed and begged me to show him my scar. In appreciation he showed me the scar on his thigh from the time he dropped an axe. We also compared appendages.

I liked the close touch of other fellows. To slide into bed alongside a warm body alleviated my loneliness. The most warmth that first year came from a brawny pal named Cole Brand. Despite his smelly feet he was roughhousingly affectionate. He was the first boy I slept all night with. He taught me to play pool, to swim the Australian crawl, and to spit intricate patterns onto a stone wall.

For my theatrical performing I gathered other admirers. Aside from acting Ariel for the official school play, I portrayed leading ladies in Archie Bianchi's impromptu melodramas. Archie improvised these lurid entertainments in the study hall on Saturday nights to amuse the boys confined to campus on weekends. Since he was addicted to opera, his plots thickened with heroines who died of unrequited passion or who stabbed villains and themselves. Sets and props were imaginary and when two female characters had to encounter, we had a problem: there was only one wig. To say nothing of a shortage of flowered bedspreads to wear. Most of the boys applauded my bravura speeches and my transvestite charms. I even received some Hershey's Kisses and Wrigley's Spearmint. So it didn't matter whether the same fellows jeered my ineptitudes at rifle drill and football. I didn't mind being called a pansy, a fruit, a fairy: they were pleasanter things to be called than a creep, a scumbag, or a shitface.

Whether or not I was being made into a man I was at least finding that I liked living among men. One morning I discovered that Hermy also lived at the school. Or nearby anyway. Because just after dawn he was standing by my bed, smiling and radiant, still three years older than I. He asked me if I was glad he had arranged my "escape" from home. He said I had to be free to experience fellowship and resourcefulness, and added, "Keep alert, be receptive. Wonders await you. Remember, adventure is not a predicament."

How lucky I was to have Hermy in my life. By the end of the first year I realized that, far from being a prison, this school in San Rafael offered me less alienation and more affection than Will Wood's dark brick house in San Francisco.

And then a year later in 1924 the military academy suddenly became a place where literature was more important than riflery. Instead of a disciplinary haven for the unwanted it became a civilian prep school, the Tamalpais School for Boys, modeled on New England institutions, tailored to the bright sons of the western well-to-do. It acquired a new tennis court and a new dormitory, grace before meals, horsemanship, no uniforms, a whole new teaching staff, and longer reading lists. There I remained until I was ignominiously removed after four years.

In that school three persons nourished my appetite for poetry. One was the new headmaster, a jovial, oratorical Yale man with a frumpy wife and three tall daughters, Dr. Williamson by name. At chapel many a morning he recited poems like "The Highwayman," "I Must Down to the Sea Again," and "General William Booth Enters Into Heaven." He introduced me to the Louis Untermeyer anthologies and the *Oxford Book of English Verse* as well as dictionaries, thesauruses, and crossword puzzles. Thanks to him I fell more deeply in love with the sounds and subtleties of the English language. I also loved Dr. Williamson because he chose me to play the piano for the chapel hymns and endured my wrong notes.

Secondly there was my classmate, James Walker Benét. In Untermeyer there were two Benéts, Stephen Vincent and William Rose. Jim was the only son of William Rose Benét, then poetry editor of what was called in those days the *Saturday Review of Literature*. Bright freckled snub-nosed Jim Benét became my adored inseparable friend and my first fellow poet. We went everywhere with locked arms. One of our favorite games was to attempt every traditional verse form and compare the results. Jim had more facility than I just as he had more literary connections. His aunt and uncle were novelists Kathleen and Charles G. Norris who lived in a hacienda in Palo Alto and entertained visitors like Alexander Woollcott and Sinclair Lewis.

Jim received long letters on blue notepaper from his father in New York, at that time in great distress over the irrational behavior of his second wife, the poet Elinor Wylie, who believed she was the reincarnation of Percy Bysshe Shelley. Ten years later, when I went to New York to become a great American writer, William Rose Benét generously gave me my first magazine publication in the *Saturday Review*: a rather flaccid lyric entitled "There is No Death."

The third inspiring person in the school provoked a sonnet a day, sometimes as many as a dozen. The cause of my literary outpouring was a stocky blond named Littlejohn, captain of the baseball team and two years older than I. I don't think I ever showed him any of my poems, but I owe to him the erotic exhilaration that writing poetry has given me ever since. Even now when I think of him I get an erection, remembering the beauty of his.

Though his legs were too short for his long torso and his chin too recessed to be ideal, Littlejohn was a golden wonder of a young man. All of his hair, including his eyelashes, armpits, and pubis, shone like white gold. Furthermore he possessed radiant skin and intoxicating body odor. More than once I wondered if he was Hermy in human guise, or some other form of angelic avatar.

In the evening he would play records for me on his windup Victrola. He especially liked Ruth Etting singing "Come To Me, My Melancholy Baby." In the morning he came to my bed before the other boys awoke and taught me the erogenous language of love. For as long as an hour he would cradle me in his arms to initiate my body to the wonders of touch and the surprises of rapture. He showed me how tender, tactile, and passionate a true comrade can be and how the body can be a temple of holy ecstasies. I wasn't sure if this was what Hermy meant by the Big Joy. But I am sure that Littlejohn inspired my lifelong faith in the redemptions of love.

This rhapsodic first romance did, alas, cause my peremptory removal from the school. By the time I was fifteen and he seventeen Littlejohn and I were dreaming of a future life together traveling around the world or living in New York where he said he had a sympathetic uncle. In fact Littlejohn spent the Christmas break in December of 1928 visiting in New York. To him there I made the mistake of writing a passionate letter declaring how much I longed to kiss his body again. A mistake, because my mother intercepted it. Ever the suspicious snooper searching for evidence to prove me a disgrace, she would rifle my drawers, cut open my locked diaries, eavesdrop on my phone calls. In this case she grabbed the letter off my desk saying she would mail it, and tore it open as soon as she left the house. She made no excuse for this betrayal. Returning home in glowering triumph she called me on the carpet in my step-father's presence, saying:

"I had no idea what a despicable squirt you are. God knows I've been a good mother to you. And this is how you reward me. Doing everything possible to make me ashamed of you. Acting like the worst kind of pervert. Carrying on with this filthy boy. You are never to see him again, do you hear?"

I had crumpled in tears. "You opened my letter! You promised to mail it!"

She went right on. "I'm at my wit's end. What am I going to do with you? You're an absolute disgrace. Obviously you can no longer be trusted. We'll have to take you out of that school at once. You will stay here at home where we can keep an eye on you at all times."

I cried out: "But he was my friend, my closest friend —"

"I don't want to hear any more about it. You've upset me enough for one day. It's all decided. You'll get over this despicable behavior or I'll settle your hash for good."

Will Wood said to me, "You should be ashamed — upsetting your mother this way. If you were my son I'd give you one helluva tanning. I'd give you the licking of your life." It was also Will Wood who said to me a month later:

"Whenever you think you're ready for it, I can fix you up with a good, safe prostitute who'll teach you the ropes."

In January I had to enroll in huge Galileo High School in the Marina. I was ordered to come directly home from school. After dinner my stepfather locked me in my room. Then he went around the entire gloomy house locking the doors and windows. He even kept a loaded pistol in a drawer beside his bed. He cautioned me always to shut the large window in my room. This was a double French window that gave onto a light well and paralleled an outside stairway of the apartment house next door. With sufficient effort any stranger could jump across into my room.

I deliberately left that window open night after night hoping for that stranger. I didn't care what he might steal as long as he stole me. I imagined him a swashbuckling hero as embraceable as Littlejohn who would free me from my imprisonment. We would sail around the world like triumphant pirates luxuriating in voluptuous capers.

By day the big public high school seemed a corral of roughnecks and squealing girls. I made few friends. One was Freddie Devereux who took me to his house to sample his mother's bathtub gin and to dance to his recording of the ballet music from *Aïda*. Sometimes I had encounters on the street, such as the perfume salesman outside the drugstore who offered me $20 to go to a hotel room with him. I was too scared to accept, but he bought me a maplenut ice-cream cone anyway.

In order to gain additional time before my evening incarceration I persuaded my mother to let me take piano lessons. Although the teacher she found for me, tweedy and bony Miss Hamm, was a devotee of Chaminade, I insisted that she let me explore Bach and the "Rhapsody in Blue" which Littlejohn had introduced me to with Paul Whiteman's original recording. A further solace I found in churches. There I could feel freer and less miserable, thinking of the Jesus whom my grandmother had adored. Jennie had died after her gallstone operation and my grandfather had surprised the town by eloping with a stern Battle Creek dietician who gave massages and high colonics.

In Grace Cathedral while swallowing his flesh and blood I asked Jesus how best to dispose of my mother and her insensitive husband. Receiving no useful answer I hoped Hermy would turn up and have some suggestions. Locked in my room at night I wrote O'Neillian dramas violent with matricide, patricide, and suicide.

Will and Olga disliked my presence in the house as much as I disliked being there. I had to endure glum dinners with them in the dining room where the walls had been painted Granny Smith green. Any dining place of that color ever since has given me an urge to puke. Olga scolded me: "Somedays you drive me crazy, you're so sullen. Can't you make some effort to be pleasant? You ought to be nicer to Will. If you just flatter him enough, you can get anything out of him."

I remembered this advice when in the fall of 1929 she went to New York to stay with Aunt Marion Ohlandt who was now a Mrs. Alwin Wild. She had been a wealthy widow when a suave Welshman married her, put her in a Park Avenue penthouse, and gave her a stainless-steel limousine in exchange for her entire inheritance.

Left at home with Will, I wondered how to try loving my enemy. Maybe if I went to work on him I could persuade him to let me go to another boarding school. I began by admiring his neckties, his golf scores, and his baritone. I buttered him up until he began to smile at me and take me to the movies. Soon I asked him if he would like to have me sleep in my mother's bed alongside his. After all, weren't we buddies now? Once ensconced beside him at night I tried more intimate blarney.

Since he wore only his open pajama coat and made a point of letting me see his manhood I questioned him about his sexual prowess. He was shamelessly proud of his substantial member and how many women it had pleased and how much my mother loved it. I praised his equipment till he glowed and preened. When I asked him if I could measure his erect cock he said, "That's enough now, son. Go to sleep."

When the stock market crashed Aunt Marion's husband jumped out of her penthouse window and Olga returned abruptly from New York. Will made me promise not to say anything to her about our intimacies and offered me a set of golf clubs. I opted for higher stakes: would he send me to the boarding school where my brother was, the Menlo School for Boys in Menlo Park? Will made one proviso: that I should take boxing lessons.

Menlo School was supposed to prepare boys for Stanford. The ancient white oaks were the only attractive thing about the place. Otherwise its primary function was to keep boys too exhausted from violent exercise to have much interest in sex or serious learning. This satisfied my sports-minded brother. But there was no chapel in the place, no theatricals, no art classes or music, only debating societies and competitive games. I worked on the school paper and tucked poems among the sports copy. I lasted only halfway through the first boxing lesson, falling to the floor in a faint. The coach didn't seem to mind. He laughed, patted me on my behind, and told me to switch to tennis.

My first roommate was named Bob Baird. He called me Roomie and gave me his white rat to sleep with. His favorite amusement

was lighting my farts with Ohio Brand matches. My second roommate, a hefty bodybuilder named Eldridge, wanted me to feel his
biceps and smell his armpits. I found more refreshment in long talks
about movies with the smartest boy in the school, wry and pudgy
Waldo Salt. In our grown-up years he and I pursued different
approaches to cinema. In those teenage times we tried to outshud-
der one another with our juiciest fantasies.

I remained at Menlo for a year and a half. As a graduation present in that summer of 1931 my Aunt Esto took me on a trip across
the USA in her Model A coupe. We looked at national parks and
local monuments all the way to the brand-new Empire State
Building. On Broadway I was enthralled at matinees of *The Green
Pastures* and *Street Scene*. Then we went to Washington to visit an
elderly cousin, Helen Nicolay, only daughter of Lincoln's secretary
John George Nicolay. Helen wrote historical novels for boys and
lived with a Miss Spofford who wrote indelicate verse. They took us
to the Freer to see the Whistlers.

In Pittsburgh we stayed with a former sorority friend of my
aunt's whose younger married sister had juicy lips, bloodshot eyes,
and no qualms. She seduced me under the orchids in the green-
house. This excursion compensated for my frustration of the summer before when at Cohasset Beach on the coast of Washington
State a smoldering nymph named Barbara Owens kept showing me
her breasts till she wearied of my timid advances and scooted off
behind the driftwood with a fullback from Seattle.

3

THE AGE OF PERPLEXITY

I HAD HOPED that college would provide some cultural exhilaration. But that was too much to expect of Stanford University in the 1930s. It had a law school, a business school, a war library, and a winning football team, but when it came to the arts its museum contained unimportant replicas and its music department consisted of the organist in the chapel. I hadn't wanted to go to Stanford in the first place. I had requested the Sorbonne or Oxford or Columbia. My mother only wanted me to learn how to get rich and meet the right people, a service Stanford was supposed to provide. She would not let me go to Berkeley because that had been my unlamented father's alma mater.

Not surprisingly the only professor teaching poetry was an arch conservative, the fierce formalist Yvor Winters. He had just published a book denouncing modern poetry as either too primitive or too decadent. He had also just been released from one of his periodic retreats in a mental hospital. On the podium he clutched the lectern savagely, his face contorting as if his innards were being stabbed. I have known other poets who had periods of lunacy, but Theodore Roethke and Robert Lowell were baby dolls compared to Winters. I believe thoroughly in being crazy, I have even written in a poem: "I pray every night to wake up crazier," but I mean being crazy *with* the cosmos not against it.

Winters denounced Shakespeare's language as too theatrical, Blake's as too blurry, Whitman's as unreadable, and song forms as trivial. He demanded that we devote our energies to the writing of heroic couplets since the couplet, he insisted, was the greatest form in English poetry. I cared too much about the riches of verse to let these strictures pass unchallenged. I persisted in asking: what about Keats? Coleridge? Carroll? He could brook no irreverence nor compromise. Like the Red Queen he merely denounced. Consequently I was inspired to write:

> A serious person is a serious business
> and serious business is a serious thing
> and serious things are very serious
> and taken seriously are dead serious
> and nothing is as serious as a serious person
> and a serious person is seriously dead.

I even concocted a spoof manifesto parodying Winters' rigid diction in which I insisted that the only form of poetry appropriate to the present age was the Anglo-Saxon; therefore poets should write in alliteration and litotes about heroic couplings. When this was published in the campus magazine, *Stanford Criteria*, Winters called me to his office and excommunicated me:

"You are to drop my class at once. I cannot bear the sight of you any longer. You have no talent of any kind, except to be silly and perverse. It is patently obvious that you will never write anything worth reading by anybody. You could not even rise to the level of Ella Wheeler Wilcox or Edgar Guest."

During my first year at Stanford I tangled with another truculent person. This was a fellow student a year older, a head taller, and a foot wider than I. A political science major who professed an aptitude for poetry, he was resolute in his pursuits.

He pursued me one evening to the third floor of Encina Hall where I had been assigned to share a room with two jocks from Oregon. Their presence deflected my pursuer that night, but the next morning he stood waiting for me outside my door. Over coffee at the union he issued me an ultimatum: because I was the most beautiful sprite he had ever seen I must come to his residence hall the following Saturday afternoon. His name was Harry Hay.

At the rendezvous in his private room he plied me with Fig Newtons, knee squeezes, and ginger ale while lecturing me on the virtues of Marxism. When I protested that I preferred poetry to politics he opened his single bed and invited me to join him there while he read aloud from his favorite verse play, *Hassan*, an Edwardian fantasy by James Elroy Flecker. Of it I recall only its many references to "the golden towers of Samarkand."

Of Harry I recall that I found his mind more fascinating than his body and his recordings of historic contraltos more impressive than his verses. But being the object of his possessiveness gave my levity the squirms. And since in that buttoned-up autumn of 1931 he was flagrantly open about both his sexuality and his communism, I was embarrassed to appear with him on campus. Stanford was scarcely his congenial school: he left before the year ended.

It was nearly fifty years later in Denver that I once again encountered Harry Hay. He was wearing long earrings, bead necklaces, and a hearing aid. He had become a garrulous activist for gay rights and a founder of the Radical Faerie movement. He embraced me fondly. But this did not erase our disharmonies, especially a disagreement about sexual personae. Regrettably he insisted on dividing humanity into hetero versus homo, not recognizing how this false dichotomy denies human spontaneity and the pansexuality of nature. He abhorred the word androgyne.

After the election of Franklin D. Roosevelt in 1932, my ultra-conservative stepfather was so convinced that murderous radicals would pillage San Francisco that he moved the family to the Monterey village of Carmel, where there were no labor unions and the only poor were artists and beachcombers. There, he said, we would hide out the Depression. This is how I came to meet Robinson Jeffers.

During the summer vacation of that year I was cast as the Page of Herodias in a production of Oscar Wilde's *Salome* in Carmel's Forest Theater. The Herodias was a raven-haired Australian named Ella Winter who had written a passionate book in praise of the Soviet Union. She was married to the retired muckraker Lincoln Steffens, who was twice her age. In fact, having finally completed his autobiography, he didn't last long past that summer, after which Ella married Donald Ogden Stewart and moved into more fashionable radical circles. I found her fiery and fascinating and so much sexier than the actress playing Salome that I sought her company after rehearsal hours.

One afternoon while we strolled on the beach Ella referred to her "intimate friend" Robin Jeffers. Then at the height of his popular fame for his verse narratives of sexual aberration in the Big Sur, Robinson Jeffers was Carmel's major celebrity. I had been trying to read his most recent work, *Thurso's Landing*, and was awed at living only a few blocks away from him. I begged Ella Winter to introduce me.

Jeffers was also famous for being reclusive. A permanent sign on his gate read: "Not at home until 4 p.m. By appointment only." Even after 4 p.m. the gate only grudgingly opened. I had been impressed by the photograph of Jeffers in *Vanity Fair* standing ruggedly Byronic against the stone wall of his tower. I did not expect to meet a man so shy of manner and so muted of speech that I could scarcely hear him. Nor did I expect a watery introverted gaze instead of the eyes of a hawk. His handshake too was unex-

pectedly soft. Most disturbing of all was the way his wife intercepted any attempt one made to address him. She would answer:
"Robin thinks this" or "We don't like that."

Ella Winter had brought a bouquet for the poet and cookies for
the wife. The wife took them both. Plainly she was guarding her
husband from female clutches, and Ella's clutches were notorious in
the community. Una Jeffers was a woman of strident chatter, plump
and maternal, adept at reducing conversation to triviality. I got little
more than an autograph out of the afternoon.

On my second visit to Tor House the atmosphere proved less
strained. Since I had come alone Una paid scant heed to a college
sophomore and went about household business, leaving me free to
converse with Jeffers. Being a melancholy Capricorn, who nursed
some kind of undeclared rage, he was scarcely a merry conversa-
tionalist. But I shared his passion for the California coast and he
was then the major poet of its geography. Besides, for me he represented an ideal of the romantic poet, one who had built his ivory
tower of stone on a dramatic promontory above the Pacific but who
also had a major publisher in New York. I was further beguiled by
his gaunt bones, beautiful fingers, and humorless intensity.

In some oblique way Jeffers seemed to enjoy my company. We
met several times during that summer to talk about poetry. He
responded to my poems more politely than Winters. I had been
overfond of adjectives and mellifluous sounds. Jeffers taught me to
value clangor in the language, the timpani of consonants, the bang
of verbs. His dictum: "A poem needs multitude, multitudes of
thoughts, all fierce, all flesh-eaters, musically clamorous."

Longing to have some of his fire and fame rub off on me, I tried
to rub against him. But he was unnerved by proximity — until the
afternoon he took me to Point Lobos. There he made me listen to
the waves pounding granite, the tide rolling pebbles, the gulls
shrieking in the wind. As we sat beside one another, staring at the
heave and splash of the sea, he became more relaxed, so much so

that when I questioned him about the tortured passions in his narratives, he admitted that he was fascinated by kinky sexuality and
unlikely violence. Then, in a surprising emotional outburst, he went
on to confess that he felt painfully trapped in the body of a man,
forced to behave in conventional human ways, when what he ached
for was the freedom of the osprey.

"The violent skies!" he said, "Or the turbulent depths, the cold
turbulent depths!" At that moment he clutched my arm so tightly
and stared seaward with such ferocity that I feared he might yank
me with him as he jumped into the icy water to drown himself. But
after a tense moment he abruptly released me, arose, and turned to
clamber back up the cliffside as if to flee the temptation. On the
drive back into Carmel he said not another word and I was not
invited again to Tor House.

In fact I did not see Robin and Una again for some fifteen years,
not until after the end of the war when Gavin Arthur and I were
invited to a luncheon party at Noel Sullivan's house in Carmel
Valley. I was shocked to discover that Jeffers had become a sullen
drunkard, while Una tried desperately to keep smiling. During the
war his poetry had fallen far out of fashion.

In my second year at Stanford I rented an apartment on the top
floor of an old white house on Salvatierra Street. It boasted a fireplace, windows opening on loquat trees, and ample space for books,
music, and visitors. I resided there the rest of my Stanford days.

That big house had four rental units. Across the hall from me
a gaunt poet from Manteca labored long to please Yvor Winters
but gave up before the year was out. Beneath him huddled a thin
brainy Greek scholar who had earned both his bachelor's and
master's degrees in three and a half years. Beneath me lived Wallace
McNulty, a tall pious-looking blond in gold-rimmed spectacles
who was studying for his doctorate in Education. He indulged
his passion for music with the largest phonograph in the house
and the most advanced recordings. Now whenever I happen to

hear Stravinksy's *Symphony of the Psalms* I vividly remember Wallace McNulty.

The night he invited me down to listen to this new acquisition he and I were alone in his candlelit room. The holy chorus had no sooner begun than McNulty drew me into the shadows behind his couch, knelt solemnly in front of me, ritually pulled down my pants, and elated my phallus with the most mouth-watering devotion it had ever experienced. Ever since then the "Laudate Dominum" of Stravinsky has given me a shudder of physical ecstasy.

When McNulty passed his orals and was packing up I suggested that if he would teach boys his virtuoso technique it would bring greater joy to mankind than any proscribed curriculum. He looked shocked and indignant.

Later that same year in a less holy ambiance I received a similar service from a fastidious classmate named Jacqueline Johnson. This took place in her Palo Alto apartment where we had been sipping sweet vermouth from jelly glasses. Since a moment before it happened she had been expounding Cubism's influence on Gertrude Stein, I reacted more with awe than rapture. Until that moment I had believed that only males performed such devotions. Now I looked at Jacqueline in a new light.

Since she was a divorcée eight years older than I who had lived in both Paris and Peking I found her so fascinating that I frequently asked her to marry me. I thought she was classy enough to impress my mother. But I did not appreciate how Jacqueline responded to my proposals with glissandos of giggling. Nor did I appreciate that she flirted shamelessly with Robert Motherwell during Professor Guerard's seminar on Art for Art's Sake. Despite my warning her that Motherwell's mother was the most notorious kleptomaniac in Portland, Oregon, she carried on an extended affair with him, claiming they only discussed philosophy. She said they had absorbing arguments about "the free choice of the good" and planned to become philosophy majors. However, Motherwell soon went to

New York where he took up painting while Jacqueline married a wealthy English surrealist named Gordon Onslow-Ford and went to live in a remodeled convent on the shore of Lake Pátzcuaro.

One twentieth-century poet whose mere name rekindles a potent memory is Ezra Pound. His work entered my life under alarming conditions during the winter quarter of my senior year.

The cultural flurries that had made Stanford bearable for the past three years had lost their novelty. I had already acted in enough plays, helped launch two campus magazines, edited the literary yearbook, and written weekly reviews of theater, books, and opera for the *Stanford Daily*. Though I was scheduled to begin rehearsal for the role of Pothinus in a spring production of *Caesar and Cleopatra*, the activity I most looked forward to was continuing modern dance work in Palo Alto with Eve Gentry, a disciple of Hanya Holm.

My thoughts were pondering my future that afternoon when they were interrupted by a sharp knock. A swarthy heavyset fellow, black-haired and frowning, loomed in the doorway. He explained that he had just moved into the vacated room across the hall. His name was Galt Hager.

Galt spoke in fawning lumps: "I applied for a room here when I found out where you lived. I wanted to be near you. I admired you from afar in Russian Realism last semester. Your poetry and your reviews in the paper, I admire them too. And I saw you dance in the Senior Follies. I want to be your friend."

Feeling vaguely threatened, I made a jesting disclaimer.

"I am serious," he insisted, continuing to stare at me. And he repeated, "I want to be your friend."

With a flourish of excuses I ushered him out. To conclude the interview decisively I had offered a handshake. It was like reaching into a bog.

Twenty minutes later Galt knocked again. This time he entered without waiting for my answer. He was carrying a book, a copy of

Ezra Pound's recently published *A Draft of XXX Cantos.* "I brought this for you. You should read it. You have such great talent as a poet, you ought to take your work more seriously. You shouldn't waste your gifts on trivial themes. The people around you don't appreciate you. They are too superficial."

Though he had pressed the book into my hands he still held onto it. He faced me with a fierce squint and panting breath. A threat of rape hovered between us. Ezra Pound served as my only shield against attack.

I don't remember how I dislodged Galt Hager and sent him away. I do remember that this was only the first of many altercations that followed when I had to strain my wits to ward off his hammering praises.

Whether or not Pound offered the correct antidote, my Stanford chums had begun to seem a glib gang who spoke of crucial matters in lame imitations of Oscar Wilde. Their other heroes were Noel Coward, Edward Lear, and Ronald Firbank. When such friends encountered Galt Hager in my quarters everybody present felt embarrassed.

And Galt persisted in invading my privacy. When he entered my sunny room storm clouds came in with him. He continued to beg for friendship, to praise every word of mine, to tell me I was a greater dancer than Nijinsky and other such flummeries.

Then came the day when Galt knocked with a fiercer urgency and burst at once into his story: "I've just learned. They've caught my father. He's in jail in El Paso. Two years ago he killed my mother and fled the country. I have only my deaf grandmother now. She has sent me to college, but that may end at any time, she says. I don't have anything to look forward to." Unnerved by this glimpse into his private world I could not think of anything to say.

He went on, "You have so many people around you. You don't know what it's like to be alone. If you'd let me be near you all the time your happy nature could heal me. We could be great friends. We could have a happy life after college. We could be poets together."

He continued in this vein as he came closer to stand implacably in front of me. Feeling cornered I lost patience. Denouncing him in words of righteous superiority that would have pleased my mother, I forbade him further access to my room.

When Galt retreated in hangdog fashion, I hoped that was the end of it. Thereafter I passed him curtly in the hall and stayed away from my room in the evening, congratulating myself that I had escaped this malevolent creature's entrapment. But I forgot that lust has its own logic.

On a warm spring night a month later when I had gone to bed earlier than usual I lay totally bare under my reading lamp. I was about to fall asleep over my book when the door surprised me by bursting open. In came Galt, slamming the door behind him, marching across the room toward my bed in the bay window, with his arms as widespread as Blake's *Glad Day*, and shouting, "You can't keep me away!"

Shock sat me upright, and my shock turned to awe. This was Galt as I had never seen him: completely nude, and in a body alarmingly beautiful. I had never suspected the warrior grace of his physique, splendidly proportioned with no laxness in it, not a blemish on his coppery skin. Most astonishing of all: his forthright and shapely penis, its throbbing power aimed directly at me. As he approached my bed my fear of him began to melt into surprised desire. Until I looked up at his face.

It wore the voracious grin of a cannibalistic gargoyle. Fear of a Desdemona fate overwhelmed me. I jumped out of bed to push him away. As I pressed against his midriff the touch of his skin electrified my fingers. But I persisted. As naked as he I pushed his nakedness across the room and out the door. I bolted it, and stood there gasping, more bewildered than relieved.

This contretemps prompted me to question my immediate future. It was the end of March, end of the winter quarter. Three months more and I would graduate with the class of 1935. Graduate into what? I was in my twenty-first year. Was it finally the moment to "run away from home" and claim the poet adventure of my life? Hermy certainly thought so. He had been prodding me for months. "Adventure, not predicament," he kept saying in my ear. "Adventure, not predicament — that's the watchword for you."

I didn't care whether I ever got a B.A. degree, whether I ever saw Stanford again. Rather than go to Carmel for a family Easter I stored my belongings in Palo Alto, closed my bank account, packed a single suitcase, and without telling anyone drove off in my blue Model A roadster toward the Tehachapi Mountains.

4

TO THE OPEN ROAD AND BACK

I WASN'T SURE where I was going. The important thing was to go. One possible goal was New York because it was there and because it claimed to include everything significant in the USA I decided to drive as far as my cash would take me. So in the cool of early spring I crossed the Mojave to Needles, then on to Flagstaff and to Gallup where the high desert was chill and blowy. Before I reached Dodge City I collided with ferocious dust blowing off the plains. I had to take refuge in auto courts to wait for a lull and try to wash the dirt out of my eyes and mouth and ears. The Joads were bound in the opposite direction.

By the time I reached Kansas City the dust had cleared and my pockets were empty. I sold my Ford to a tobacco-chewing crook in a used car lot for a humiliating sum and walked to the eastern edge of the city carrying my cardboard suitcase. There for the first time in my life I held out my thumb toward oncoming traffic. I tap-danced to keep warm and appear insouciant. Was this adventure, not predicament?

After a couple of short rides with Missouri farmers I flagged a shiny coupe. The burly man at the wheel asked me if I could drive. "Sure," I said. "Drive me to Culver Military Academy in Indiana," he said as he slid across the seat and fell into a heavy snore.

After I crossed the Wabash at Terre Haute he woke up and revealed himself as the football coach at Culver. He had been on an all-night binge after a Golden Gloves tournament. When he learned that I was a poet he invited me into his digs at the military school, gave me a Dr. Pepper, and made me read aloud from his favorite book: *The Prophet* by Kahlil Gibran. This seemed to alleviate his hangover. When I further entertained him by reciting "The Owl and the Pussycat" and singing "Mad Dogs and Englishmen" he assembled a group of athletic cadets to hear me read from his copy of *Great Poems of the Western World*. This initiated me into the arctic experience of reading poetry to a defiantly indifferent audience. The coach, however, was so delighted that he invited me to spend the night. His wide snoring bulk on his narrow bed allowed me only the thinnest edge of it so that I had to cling to him to keep from falling off. I even tried clinging to his penis but it offered no substantial support. Next morning the coach drove me to the Fort Wayne highway, bought me ham and eggs in a greasy spoon, slapped me on the back and barreled off.

When further rides dumped me south of Albany I decided to bus the rest of the way into Manhattan. Once in the big city I phoned a college cohort, Jim Sandoe, under whose direction the year before I had acted in *Doctor Faustus* and *Hay Fever*. He was studying theater history at Columbia for his master's. He booked me into his dormitory and on my first night took me to the talked-about new play, *Waiting for Lefty*. I did not inform my mother of my whereabouts. Let her worry! I wasn't proving to her that I wasn't a sissy, I was proving to myself how far a sissy could go.

From 116th Street I rode the subway down to the Battery, went into the office of the American Export Lines and asked for a job.

This was not quite as dumb as it sounds. On my voyage to Manila the previous summer I had been nice to a dowdy lady named Mrs. Rosenbalm. When she revealed that her husband was an executive of a New York steamship company I thought it shrewd to obtain her address in New Jersey and to make genteel passes at her homely daughter. Mrs. Rosenbalm urged me to keep in touch. I sent her a Christmas card, wrote to her from an Arizona motel and phoned her from the Columbia campus. Her husband must have had a guilt button she could push. Though he hemmed and hawed, cross-questioned me and frowned, in the end he offered me a job on one of his passenger cargo ships. The S.S. *Excalibur* was due to sail in a week's time to many ports around the Mediterranean. This good luck happened in the era before strong maritime unions, otherwise such a rookie landlubber would have been laughed out of the office.

During the week before the ship sailed from Hoboken I was assigned temporary duty in the mess of the maintenance crew, a profane bunch of huskies who found hilarious my efforts to serve them meals and clean up after them. I survived this humiliation by laughing with them and getting my butt pinched. In my bunk at night I slept with the only book I had carried with me from California, Emerson's *Essays*, in the Everyman edition. The pages most heavily underlined were those of "Self Reliance."

By the time the ship sailed I had been outfitted with a white mess jacket and black bow tie to participate in the ceremonies of the steward department. I was to serve the passengers as busboy, purveyor of liquids, and backup waiter. The day before the *Excalibur* lifted anchor I mailed a letter to Olga boasting matter-of-factly that I was now a member of the crew of an ocean liner about to cross the Atlantic on a long voyage.

In my quarters ten waiters and cooks were assigned to double bunk beds and lockers. I had to spar with an Italian waiter named Fernando who would flash his erect member at me, saying "Look what you do to me!" I had also to outwit the pink-cheeked pastry cook who wanted to stuff his ladyfingers up my ass. The purser had warned me: "At sea keep your pecker in your pants. Whatever you do, do it ashore."

I loved being at sea, loved the vistas, the sense of inhabiting a traveling island. Carrying breakfast or cocktail trays up the breezy outside companionways to the staterooms required tightrope dexterity. I had to deliver special formulas to the Captain who suffered from a queasy stomach.

I often lingered to chat in some of the staterooms, especially with dancer and mime Angna Enters, with an Italian jurist in gaudy pajamas who plied me with Strega, and an elderly woman doctor from Florida who was bound for Iran to persuade the Shah to ban the wearing of the veil by Persian women. Her name was Dr. Rosalie Slaughter Morton. She confided that in her retirement she planned to write the story of her life struggles against the patriarchy of the AMA.

But the most interesting fellow voyager was the stocky blond Dane who slept in the upper bunk next to mine. I guessed he was no ordinary seaman: he was reading *Flowering Judas* by Katherine Anne Porter. He admitted that he went intermittently to sea for the sheer joy of it. On land he had a career as a foreign correspondent. His name was Emil Opffer.

When I admitted having read Porter's book, Emil told me he knew Katherine Anne personally. He spoke of other literary acquaintances, especially of Hart Crane with whom he used to live whenever he stayed in New York. He confided that his seagoing adventures had been the source of Crane's work *Voyages*, which was in effect a love poem to Emil. When I pressed him he admitted that he had been Hart Crane's "special sweetheart." I could understand why Emil attracted Crane: he was as blithely uncontaminated as Billy Budd. When he spoke about Hart Crane's suicide leap into the Gulf of Mexico in 1932, tears ran down his ruddy cheeks. He said Crane had died for love of him, that he had wanted to wed himself to the sea.

On our voyage around the Mediterranean Emil enriched my shore leave extravagantly. He could not bear to hold onto money. In Marseilles he introduced me to *pastis* and took me to a *cine bleu*. In Genoa he took me to the birthplace of Columbus and treated me to my first hot zabaglione. In Alexandria he took me through the catacombs and then to a brothel. In Jerusalem he took me to the Holy Sepulcher and rented a suite for us at the new King David Hotel.

By the time we were back in Hoboken we had become firm buddies. Delighted to have found such a lively fellow adventurer I stood ready to follow Emil wherever he wanted to go. Where he first wanted to go was Washington, D.C. And he took me there on the very next bus. He explained that he had to file stories to *Politiken* in Copenhagen to make sure of receiving his retainer fee. To my surprise he held membership in the National Press Club. He obtained a pass for me so I could use the typewriters and sign for food and drinks. Spurred by working journalists around me I wrote an article about Mussolini's Black Shirts with special reference to a popular gelato that celebrated Italy's recent acquisition of an African colony.

Emil and I were bedded in the comfortable guest room of his friends, a jolly Danish couple who owned a Scandinavian restaurant near Dupont Circle. We talked of renting an apartment of our own. But one morning Emil said he was broke and would have to go to sea again. Did I want to sign on with him for Buenos Aires? Despite how much I enjoyed being his comrade, I had to recognize that I could not keep pace with someone whose heart belonged more to the waves of the sea than to any human being. Besides, I wanted to test my landlubber wings in New York.

Before sailing to South America Emil introduced me to Crane's literary friends Waldo Frank, Newton Arvin, and especially Malcolm Cowley, who persuaded *The New Republic* to print my essay, "Abyssinian Ice Cream." This heightened my expectation of a shining literary career in New York. But pursuing stories assigned to me I quickly learned that journalism would never be my forte. It was not in my nature to pay more attention to actualities than to unlikelihoods.

I pounded Manhattan pavements, combed want ads, marched in protest parades. Those were the years when hip youngsters sang the "Internationale" at rallies in Madison Square Garden. I also took classes in modern dance at the Humphrey-Weidman studio on West 19th Street. I loved the leaping of bodies and the percussion of bare feet. Charles Weidman was rehearsing a men's group for a production based on the Paul Bunyan story that would feature José Limón in the title role. At the beginning of rehearsals I was in the corps. So was Milo Cody.

Milo was a potent young buck from Des Moines with a tough grace, a Marxist mind, and the heart of a lamb. The first time we sat side by side at a rehearsal break Milo appraised me intently, then awarded me a spacious grin. He told me he was disgusted with the loftiness of people like Martha Graham. He wanted to take directly to the people dances that dealt with urgent realities. He was forming a group of his own to perform antiwar pieces on weekends for workers' organizations. Did I want to join him? How could I refuse this endearing dynamo? For that matter, how could I refuse his invitation to share the bed in his unheated loft?

For his troupe Milo managed to lure four women from Doris Humphrey's class and to obtain funding from the WPA Dance Project. His enthusiasm won us engagements at union halls in the Bronx, in Brooklyn, and the East Side. Our most popular number was called "Gas Attack," performed in gas masks, and our best audience the Jewish Women for Peace. Though Milo had finesse as a performer, his choreography was relentlessly emphatic.

As for the Paul Bunyan project, Charles Weidman dismissed me for dragging my feet in the presto leaps. This forced me to acknowledge that my innate tempo was too relaxed for rapid counts. Furthermore I had to admit I did not possess resilient enough lift and extension to become a first-rate dancer. "Don't be sad about it,"

Hermy whispered to my inner ear. "Dance with words. You were born a poet. Dance with life. Celebrate the dance of everything."

In time I also had to acknowledge the unnecessary discomfort of life in Milo's drafty loft. His habit of pulling the covers off me every night tended to chill the illusion of romance. Whenever he did happen to notice me, he was bluntly tender, and his sexual force remained as dynamic as his jeté. But I suspected that Milo would always love the exhilaration of dancing more than any relationship until, perhaps, his limbs stiffened and he got married and had a brood of sturdy kids back in Des Moines.

At the National Vaudeville Club in Times Square I rented a minimal room next to Jim Benét's. He wanted me to go to Spain with him but I hadn't yet convinced myself that I could survive in my own country. Macy's wouldn't give me a job but Gimbel's would. I worked in its unliterary book department through the Christmas season. When Olga and Will came to New York during December to stay at the Plaza, I enjoyed refusing money from them. Olga frowned at my defiant life, "You can't go on like this, clerking in a department store."

My ego swaggered as I replied, "On the first of January I go to Winter Park, Florida, to ghostwrite the autobiography of a woman surgeon."

It was true: I had been corresponding persuasively with Dr. Rosalie Slaughter Morton. She had offered me an amanuensis job at minimal pay, but it included a cottage of my own and a canoe to go with it. When I arrived in central Florida Dr. Morton made it clear that she not only wanted to be known as the exclusive author of her life story, she also wanted me to write up her polemic against the Shah. In Teheran she had told him a thing or two and had actually ripped off one surprised woman's veil.

The old lady had egomania to burn and she kept it afire night and day. Beginning with her Virginia blue-blood heritage she had a lengthy history of battling antifeminist prejudice as she fought her way to the top of her profession. Despite the stresses of recording her daily reminiscence, I enjoyed the challenge and the Florida winter. Dr. Morton recognized that she had a bargain ghostwriter in tow, but not wanting her neighbors to discover what I was doing she introduced me locally as a long lost nephew from way out West. I completed her two books in four months' time. They were published the following year under her authorship: *A Woman Surgeon* and *A Doctor's Holiday in Iran*.

Occupying a cottage away from the main house allowed me an illusion of liberty: I could row on the everglady lakes, ride the bus to Orlando, entertain visitors. One afternoon when the young Episcopal chaplain from Rollins College sprawled on my cot browsing in Joyce's *Ulysses*, at my door appeared a singular form of gypsy scholar. He was a long-haired bifocaled old boy in a rumpled linen suit, his pockets filled with garlic cloves which he constantly nibbled. From these pockets he also brought forth sheaves of pamphleteering that he had published at his "headquarters for universal enlightenment" in Geneva. Carlton Chilton was his name. He had the manner and the accent of a dilapidated Harvard dropout.

He also possessed the verbosity of a fanatic. He was proselytizing his version of jolly Buddhism as the only possible salvation for the decline of the west. From his fistful of pamphlets he extracted one smallish envelope. "You," he said, "look like someone who will appreciate this. Young man, here are the ten bulls of Zen Buddhism. Understand these and you will be liberated."

At this point the chaplain fled, leaving me alone with this endearing zany who not only enlightened me amusingly but also sang Appalachian folk songs to the mandolin he carried. Before he left he gave me another gift: a photograph of a mossy bust. "You are a poet. Here for you is a picture of Shelley. Doesn't he look like someone from another world who is just about to return?"

I was sorry when Chilton departed for Sarasota. I framed Shelley and kept him above my desk. But the ten pictures of the gradually

disappearing bull flummoxed me. In that spring of 1936 Zen
Buddhism seemed more esoteric than *The Secret Doctrine* of
Madame Blavatsky.

In May Will called from San Francisco to say that my mother
was in the hospital being operated on for complications from a
blockage in her colon. He was sending me a train ticket. When I
reached California her condition had not improved: cancer was
detected in the digestive system and a series of treatments pre-
scribed. I decided to use that forced summer in the west to complete
my B.A. at Stanford. I studied Dante in Italian, Baudelaire in
French, and body English around the swimming pool.

In the fall of 1936 a second operation for Olga demanded a long
hospitalization. Since Will dreaded living alone, he insisted I stay
and share his apartment in the Huntington on Nob Hill. By now I
knew how to manipulate him and could even listen deadpan to his
boast that Alf Landon would defeat Roosevelt by a landslide in
November. Twice a day I drove him to the hospital and nightly
dined with him on room-service lamb chops. Later I would escape to
my own indulgences, most often to Jack Sowden's unkempt mansion
on Turk Street where he oversaw a nightly salon of eclectic revelry.

One seldom saw Jack Sowden eat anything. He was rich enough
to live on a continuous diet of whisky, gentlemen callers, whiplash
repartee, and sexual sport with his sister. A brash and bawdy host,
he would entertain entire football teams or squadrons of the Navy,
as well as celebrities in transit like Ramon Novarro or Vladimir
Horowitz.

One of his visitors was Howard Greer, a flourishing fashion
designer from Hollywood with a mirthful eye and a flamboyant
style. Howard called me his "Venetian Glass Nephew" and invited
me to join him for a weekend at Highlands Inn in Carmel. We got
along so merrily on the Highlands that Howard invited me down to
his new Toluca Lake home in Los Angeles. Though Nebraska born,
with a farm boy's awe at his own success, Howard Greer's wit was

trenchant, his sense of beauty classic, his daily life a high comedy. He not only dressed movie stars; his clients also included maharanis, duchesses, and Mrs. Louis B. Mayer. A dinner party he gave for me, attended by Travis Banton, Walter Plunkett, Orry-Kelly, and Edith Head, provided a sparkling education in dressmaker camp. I remember the gardenias in the soup. Howard was amused by everything including himself, but his breezy world of self-mocking artifice was no place for a poet still in quest of a reality.

By Christmas Olga was released from the hospital and Will took her to Arrowhead Springs before they returned to Carmel. I took myself to New York via the Sunset Limited to New Orleans, where during Carnival and Lent I lived in a mouldy courtyard. There I wrote a short novel called *My Malevolent Star* which probed the enigma of an intimidating character like Galt Hager. I had not come to terms with Galt's invasion of my life. Questions still haunted me: what was his true history? had he really been an evil presence? had my rejection ruined his life?

Months after I had finished the manuscript and resettled in New York I received out of the blue a letter from Galt forwarded to me from Stanford. It said: "I apologize for writing to you, but I thought you might like to know that I live now in Honolulu. It is paradise here. I work for the morning newspaper, the *Star Bulletin*. I am married to Antoinette and we have two boys. The first-born is called James after you. He is a very beautiful child."

This decided me not to seek a publisher for that novel. Even so I was still obsessed with novel-writing. I began another that autumn, one that tried to amplify my escapade with Howard Greer into a bittersweet heterosexual romance. Fortunately, this thinly plotted exercise in deception was spurned by the publishing world.

If you can't create, criticize. In 1938 I was reviewing sometimes three or four, even five, novels a week for Irita Van Doren's Sunday "Books" section of the *New York Herald Tribune*. My reviews were published under a set of pseudonyms assigned to me by Irita to make it appear that she had a wide field of critical minds on her staff. For verbal amusement I tried to give a different style to each of my aliases. It was tacitly understood that all novels were to receive qualified praise, well-advertised novels unqualified raves.

I lived at that time in the attic of a rooming house on East 10th Street with Barbara Perkins, who was recovering from a sadistic novelist named Raymond Holden. Lovely but squeamish Barbara proved too masochistic a lover for my non-macho embrace and she moved on to a series of painful unions. Like many a penurious reviewer I gobbled booze and cheese at literary cocktail parties where I met novelists and critics and a few popular poets. I looked forward to shaking hands with Edna St. Vincent Millay whose sonnets had prompted my own to Littlejohn. But she pulled her hand away and spilled her martini on the Persian carpet. Her eyes looked like she wept a lot.

Though I met other poets of the thirties, from Delmore Schwartz to Phyllis McGinley, I failed to find a congenial mentor. Patchen fascinated me, but Miriam did her best to squelch the fascination. e. e. cummings disappointed me the most: instead of a mischievous troubadour one met a decorous Unitarian minister. In Manhattan I actually felt closer to Whitman than to any living writer. I would fancy him sitting beside me in an Automat sharing a yawp or two as we watched the ebb and flow of humanity. Like Hermy, Walt urged me to praise, not disparage, to recognize all men as potential comrades, and to understand how poetry is an art of sexual joy.

In the spring of 1939 Olga suffered a relapse: the cancer had invaded her kidneys. During the early summer my brother and I sat out two months of vigil with Will as we awaited Olga's demise. We were confined to a Pacific Heights apartment where only the view of ships sailing out of the Golden Gate alleviated the claustrophobia. To Will's disgust, Nicholas had become a Quaker and worked in Washington for the League Against War and Fascism. Will scolded him for not appreciating how Hitler was teaching those damn Jews a lesson. Will scolded both of us for how much worry we had caused Olga over the years, as though that was the reason for her doom.

Despite her waning strength my mother's vanity had not followed suit. When I sat at her bedside one afternoon she lamented: "Think of it. August 27th I will be fifty years old, isn't that terrible? I can't face getting old. I will have to have a face-lift or I won't be able to go on."

Will had given her nothing to live for but her self-indulgence. He had barred everything stimulating from her life and despite his vaunted potency, he had never given her what she most wanted: a baby daughter. She had often fantasized the baby girl she would name Louise. I was surprised at my belated sympathy for this denunciatory parent who now appeared so feeble and deluded.

During Olga's final days my Aunt Esto turned up at the Vallejo Street apartment. Due perhaps to her own precarious health she had become a fervent Christian Scientist. She insisted that she bring her practitioner to Olga's bed. I pled with her not to interfere. Olga's death would mean my liberation. Besides, as I told my aunt, this was Olga's escape from her suffocating marriage. Didn't Esto remember what she had told me about her brother's desire to escape from his marriage — by joining his friend Justin in death?

Olga never had to have her face lifted. She died two days before her fiftieth birthday. These were her farewell words to me: "How long are you going to go on wasting your life? Will you never settle down and be something? God knows I gave you every opportunity. I guess you kids have just been spoiled rotten. . . . Oh, don't talk about a war. That's just your excuse. There won't be any war."

Despite this assurance a week later Hitler went ahead and invaded Poland. Will took Olga's death as a personal affront. "Godammit. Why was she taken away from me? Didn't I give her everything she ever wanted?"

The months following Olga's cremation proved more bewildering than liberating. Nicholas returned to Washington and I moved out as soon as I could. To compensate for years of having my sexuality under wraps I felt I deserved some lustful abandon. Besides, we were living suddenly in a threatening world and desperation was in the air. I rented a little house where I tried holding Sowden salons of my own. I haunted bars and drag clubs: The Black Cat, The Red Lizard, the Blue Parrot, The Purple Onion, The Beige Room, as well as, of course, various Turkish baths. I experienced hangovers and gonorrhea, crabs and anal warts, lighthearted romance and profound gloom. When in a mood of revulsion I realized I had fixed up my cottage the way my mother would have liked it, I sold everything and moved to a one-room apartment in the Tenderloin where I wrote haikus and planned Kafkaesque novellas.

Pearl Harbor interrupted my uneasy dalliance with a summons from the Selective Service System. When ordered to report for induction at 8 a.m. on an upcoming Tuesday, I pondered what to do. I couldn't countenance killing fellow men, whoever they were, yet I didn't possess the single-mindedness of my brother who as a registered Quaker could claim Conscientious Objector status.

It was a chilly morning at the Induction Center on lower Market Street. I and three hundred other young men were told to take off all our clothes, shoes included. Both my balls and my heart shriveled. On orders we moved in single file from desk to desk being questioned, measured, tabulated. I was conspicuous in the line because I was the only one carrying something. This was a letter addressed "To Whom It May Concern" and had been written by a quack psychiatrist. I had paid him to say that I was unfit to kill Japs and Nazis because I preferred butterflies to bazookas.

I had hoped to give this letter to an official when I first arrived and so be quickly excused. But no one would look at it, no one would take it. Finally the single file reached a trio of superior officers who were examining the inductable genitals. When I faced a bullish colonel, he took hold of my penis, looked under it, pulled up my testicles, looked under them, made me turn around and bend over to show him my asshole. Then he asked me whether I had any sexual diseases. In desperation I offered him the letter. Much to my relief he took it. But he frowned when he read it, then passed it to his associates who muttered over it and glared at me. The would-be soldier behind me said, "What's the matter? What's wrong with you?"

What was wrong with me? There I stood shivering in front of the United States Army brass who held my questionable life in their hands. When the colonel turned to me again he barked, "We don't want any goddamn fruitcakes corrupting the boys in this man's army. You are a disgrace to your country in its hour of peril. Get going!"

I burst into a fit of sneezes and went sheepishly to get my clothes.

Having gained my 4F status I was relieved but intimidated. At the beginning of the war everyone I encountered asked when I was going to fight for my country. I decided to move to Los Angeles where I knew no one. Having promised the draft board to engage in some civilian war work, I put in an uneasy stint at Douglas Aircraft only to be dismissed for mechanical ineptitude. I lived on Pinehurst Road behind Grauman's Chinese Theater in a thin-walled studio populated by ravenous moths and carpenter ants. Next door a buxom Belgian blonde named Bettina pursued a raucous affair with William Faulkner. Howard Greer was in London with Special Services.

Having no one of my own to talk to I took the Wilshire bus out to Westwood and consulted a Hungarian psychiatrist named Lydia Sicher who was both gaunt and blunt. She wasted no time in telling me I had a mother complex and that all homosexuals were obsessed with sex. This didn't help matters. Being an Adlerian, however, she believed in dealing immediately with any problem.

"What," she asked me, "would you like to achieve to prove your mother wrong?"

"Be a successful playwright," I heard myself saying.

"Before you can be successful," said the Adlerian, "you first have to be a playwright."

This provoked my departure a month later for another assault on New York City. I lived in a dark back room of the old Hotel Brevoort at Washington Square and enrolled for drama classes at the New School for Social Research on 12th Street. Now instead of imagining Brentano's window filled with my novels, I dreamed of my SRO signs, a Pulitzer prize, and the unqualified praise of George Jean Nathan.

In the marrow of my being I knew that I was a poet and always would be, but there were times during the war when I did fear being alone and being laughed at. Was I beginning to look like someone from another world who was about to return? To keep in touch with Hermy I went often to "Smoky Mary's" on 46th Street, which Virgil Thomson had introduced me to: the Anglican Church of St. Mary the Virgin where the incense was awesome, the vestments exquisite, and the music divine. I had long since dumped dogma but I still believed that Jesus was the grandest sissy of all time.

Sitting in a pew I would often hear Hermy whispering, "Holy, holy, holy. Everything is holy. What are you doing to persuade men of their holiness? How's your fieldwork for the Big Joy? Did you forget that life is an ever-expanding audacity?"

I did forget. The first sentence of my book, *Seeing the Light* of 1977, reads: "When I was thirty my greatest consolation was the thought of suicide." On my thirtieth birthday in November 1943 I dined in a clattering cafeteria, my only company a copy of Rilke's *Sonnets to Orpheus* and a letter from Des Moines informing me that Milo Cody had been killed in action in the Pacific. What could poetry do to make men prefer loving to killing?

My literary life seemed also to be perishing. No magazines would print my poems and my best novel — a picaresque nightmare called *The Hitchhiker* — had been rejected by six publishers. As for being a dramatist on Broadway I had difficulty persuading even an obscure group that met in the YWCA to give one play of mine a staged reading. It was called *A Love for Lionel*. Like Peer Gynt,

Lionel searched the world for ideal love. Unlike Peer Gynt, when Lionel returned to the hometown girl of his youth she was bored by his advances. I have wondered whether this denouement was influenced by my actress friend at the New School. Whenever I tried to kiss Katrina Bishop she yawned in my face. If you wanted to get her into bed, you had to penetrate a barrage of yawns. My other sidekick at the night classes, a lusty reporter named Leon Mohr, yakked too much ever to yawn. Anyway he didn't believe in going to bed with people he liked.

One elderly personage who appreciated my writing and even rewarded me for it was a lady named Mrs. Henry White Cannon, widow of a late president of the Chase National Bank. She employed me as her secretary during 1944 and for a while I lived on the fourth floor of her brownstone mansion on East 62nd Street. Technically she lived there alone — with a cook, two maids, a chauffeur, a man who came once a week to wind all the clocks, a regular window cleaner, a chimney sweep, and a pest controller who disinfected the entire building and dislodged pigeons from the roof. In the parlor hung Monet haystacks, in the elevator a nubile Renoir.

My major duty was to confront the daily mound of mail beseeching donations to worthy causes, an invasion all rich people have to expect. Surprisingly Mrs. Cannon contributed solely to causes and politicians dedicated to undermining her capitalist security. Her father had been a liberal senator from Ohio while she herself financed the Mary McLeod Bethune College for black women in Daytona Beach. My mornings were occupied deciding who got money and how much, who got the subscription seats at the Philharmonic and the Metropolitan Opera, and who got invited to dinner with whom.

Mrs. Cannon had her own way of encouraging individual artists. She did not support them at work, she rewarded their work when completed. Thus after I showed her in January of 1945 the most recent play of mine called *Summer Fury* she took me to the

Cosmopolitan Club for luncheon and when we had finished our *blanc mange* she slipped me an envelope with a check in it for $500. Perhaps she responded to the play's subject matter: the tragic fate of a poor Chicano boy in Los Angeles victimized by prejudice and police. I had written it as an exercise in melodrama for John Gassner's class. What sparked its tragedy was my own sense of being a victimized outsider in a time of destructive madness.

This play was the first of mine to gain any recognition. Not only was it included in "The Best Short Plays" of that year, but the Dramatists Alliance of Stanford bestowed a prize on it. They planned to premiere it as part of a theater festival in the upcoming summer and invited me to attend.

Thus was I returned to my unloved campus and to San Francisco. Will had been stricken with angina and gone to live with a sister in Portland. Nicholas was still interred in a C.O. camp in the San Bernardino mountains. I took temporary refuge in Ruth Witt-Diamant's basement, intending to return to New York at the end of summer. But five years passed before I got back to the Hotel Brevoort to retrieve the trunks I had stored in its basement, only to find a brand-new apartment tower erected on the site. What delayed me so long? Three major events: President Truman dropped a bomb on Japan, Hitler committed suicide, and I dove into a whirlpool of maverick poets.

5

PODS OF POETS

ART WAS BOILING over. Once the war ended artists could drop their uniformities and take up free play again. In San Francisco poetry sang out for all to hear.

The prime torchbearer for public poetizing was a zesty Irish songbird named Madeline Gleason who loved to read poetry aloud and hear it read. In 1946 she bullied museums, galleries, and bookshops into sponsoring poetry readings. These evenings she organized like song recitals presenting four, six, even eight poets on a single program like a set of musical numbers. Her greatest difficulty was to restrain readers from going beyond their brief time limits. The least talented always went on the longest.

Madeline dyed her hair geranium red and wore scarlet lipstick. She lived on Telegraph Hill with a teacher lady, an orange tabby, and a red velvet armchair to curl up in. Devoted to tea and whisky and the Virgin Mary she moved at a brisk skedaddle, dashing off verses in a licketysplit scrawl. Since she could never sit still in an office, she relished her job as a runner in the financial district delivering stocks and bonds and official documents. It kept her out in the air and was simple-minded enough to allow her to versify in her head while she trotted along Montgomery Street. Sometimes she was so absorbed in a stanza she took securities to the wrong bank.

Madeline opened a vein that provided the source of San Francisco's future as a major center of poetry and poetry performance in America. She brought poets to the public, the poets met one another privately. Robert Duncan had a Libertarian coterie in Berkeley. Kenneth Rexroth held weekly gatherings in his San Francisco flat where poets read to other poets and where Kenneth told them what was politically correct and what to do about it. He pressured a reporter from *Harper's* to promote the idea of a San Francisco renaissance of the arts. When the magazine called the movement "Sex and Anarchy" Kenneth exploded.

Kenneth Rexroth often exploded. Robert Duncan called him The Terrible Tempered Mister Bangs. You could never predict what might ignite Kenneth's rage, or what could soothe it. You might phone him with a simple question only to encounter a tornado of denunciation; the next morning he would call back in a tone of crusty honey: "Hello dearie, this is Glinda the Good!"

Kenneth once retaliated by calling Duncan Mother Scold. After all, they were both Capricorns, and Capricorns are notably testy with one another. By the same token Kenneth had iffy relations with Henry Miller, Alan Watts, Charles Olson, Stan Brakhage, Robert Bly — to name but a few other Capricorns.

Conversations with Kenneth never went smoothly. His demeanor was that of a crotchety cactus. He began any exchange with a grumble that sounded like gruff indifference until some fancy would tickle him and his snicker would grow into a cackle. He would nudge one's ribs and deliver yet another of his japes: "That guy may be considered a pure genius in Iowa City, but everyone else knows he has two cocks — one for women and one for men."

Kenneth's exaggerations moved from the lofty to the trashy. From one conversation alone I noted in my journal the following: "The only poet worth reading in bed with a beautiful woman is Li Po . . . All juveniles are written by lesbians with three names . . . The two deadliest foes of literature in New York are Blanche Knopf and Bennett Cerf . . . When James Farrell goosed Muriel Rukeyser in the Gotham Book Mart she knocked him out cold . . . Thomas Merton can't write a poem unless another monk diddles him with some thorns . . . and so on." No wonder that Doubleday, to obviate libel suits, insisted that Kenneth's autobiography be subtitled *A Novel*.

Kenneth embroidered reminiscence like a roughshod Proust claiming to have been everywhere and done everything. I regret that he seldom allowed into his writing the spontaneous nuttiness of his impromptu talk. Instead he created an image of himself as a rugged man of nature usually observing some scenic harmony and affirming that nature is grand and man is vile. This self-portrait of a sophisticated Thoreau excluded his obstreperous madness. All poets can be heir to schizophrenia given the difficulty of harmonizing private vision with the daily mire. Often enough this has led them to the clinic, the asylum, or the morgue. Kenneth was tough enough to survive the perils of his calling and the pitfalls of his paranoia.

In the forties and fifties Kenneth played father to many young poets of San Francisco. They were the sons he never had. He was their Poundian arbiter, teaching them rebellious anarchies in society and abstract formalities in art. For me Kenneth was less a father than an eccentric uncle, one whose visits were looked forward to with as much dread as eagerness. But I enjoyed the hefty snorts he would emit when he hugged me. He was a great snorter.

When his wife Martha had her affair with Robert Creeley, Kenneth blamed me for it because I had found Creeley an apartment on Telegraph Hill where the lovers could tryst. Once when I was there Kenneth stood outside on the Montgomery Street steps shouting up at the windows: "Come out of there, James, you pimp, you strumpet, come out or I'll shoot you!" until the whole neighborhood was roused. And yet two days later Terrible Tempered Mister Bangs brought me a copy of *In Defense of the Earth*, affectionately inscribed.

For decades Robert Duncan and I were linked by literary devotions and convivial celebrations. The day after his death in 1988 I wrote this poem:

He was called Bear by friend and lover
when first I met him forty years ago.
He called himself a bearish magicker
and tossed abracadabras out of his topknot.

He was a ravenous bear, an irascible bear,
a garrulous guffawing grandiloquent bear.
More claw than paw, more Grizzly than Teddy,
he could bear no nonsense from Goldilocks.

Tireless honey-hunter in the forest of fancy
and rhapsodic custodian of the language tree,
he could bear witness to roots and branches,
he could bear fruits of versatile abundance.

Constructing a constellation of lofty lights
to bedeck his circus of bearish magick
he became the Ursa Major of his own star system.
He remains an Ursa Major to bear in mind brightly.

Duncan was certainly the most prominent bear in my life. That his body was especially hirsute prompted his nickname, and he took the bear as a lifelong totem. His mouth was too small for a bear: one of the smallest I have ever seen on a man. But it discharged enormous quantities of verbiage from an unusually large head. Since he had one nearsighted eye and one farsighted eye, it was often difficult to know whether he was looking at you or at the wall behind you. Sometimes when he changed focus the discarded eye would wander off to a side wall, and he would remind one of Cyclops. When sexually attracted to anyone both eyes would come into fierce focus. His stare could be relentless.

This I experienced early in our acquaintance. When I was living temporarily in a Sausalito cottage I asked Robert to come to dinner and spend the night. He was then living alone in Berkeley and Pauline Kael was staying with me. The small guest room of the house was on a level below the main floor. Before turning in for the night I went down to take Robert a pillow. The door stood ajar. I entered to find Robert naked except for his scivvies. He came toward me focusing his greedy stare, then grabbed hold of me.

"You don't want to sleep with Pauline, you know you don't. Look at me!" He moved back to drop his shorts and reveal his erect cock. "I want you! You want me, don't you? I can give you a better fuck than Pauline can!"

This encounter was not unlike the time in Yellowstone Park when I was confronted by a huge brown bear advancing rapidly toward the sandwich in my hand. This time I had a similar reaction — abrupt flight.

After the Sausalito evening Robert met a young painter, Jess Collins, with whom he settled into a dense domesticity that lasted for thirty-seven years, a life cluttered with paintings, books, cats, souvenirs, and a miscellaneous stream of poets.

Duncan was the first poet I had ever met who walked as if clad in Apollonic mantle. Whether his poems were great mattered not a whit: he was obviously great at being a poet. As Madeline Gleason said, "I am not always sure what Robert is talking about, but he always sounds grand."

I marveled how often Robert would come up my stairs and without even an acknowledging hello would sit down wherever, on a cat or a film can, and begin to write furiously line after line in the notebook he always carried, puffing innumerable cigarettes like a possessed choo-

choo, oblivious of everything until he had finished. Then he would immediately read aloud what he had written in his rushed incantatory voice, whether anyone was listening or not. His conversation was a bewildering tour of hermetic philosophy, astrology, linguistics, Celtic myth, the Zohar, Whitehead, medieval history, family history, and many other zones freely retranslated by his mental hopscotch.

Besieged from all sides by poets eager to be heard, Madeline Gleason called on Robert and me for help in arranging programs. No local institution would do more for poetry than hire an occasional big name, so we functioned as casual impresarios under the rubric of The Poetry Guild until an appreciative professor at San Francisco State, Ruth Witt-Diamant, established the Poetry Center on the campus. This still flourishes as a major sponsor and an archive.

Of the private reading groups the most rewarding for me was a sextet who called themselves Devotees of the Maiden and who honored the Muse with monthly feasts of food and imagination. Besides Madeline, Duncan, and myself the other members were Jess, Helen Adam, and Eve Triem.

By this time Robert and Jess had moved to a cottage on the hillside above Stinson Beach. When I was suffering midlife sorrows of befuddlement they gave me refuge in the attic. Between his paste-ups and paintings Jess grew lettuces and artichokes. Robert made stained glass windows out of plastics and printed *Faust Foutu* on his Enkidu Press. There were temperamental cats, Monarch butterflies, music of Stravinsky and Kurt Weill, surprising foods, poet visitors. I found a house nearby that I wrote of in *Tidings*.

But our friendship began to unravel when Duncan decided to abandon free-flowing seaside life for mainstream literary life. He announced a campaign to make himself conspicuous to the critical establishment and its key pundits. He felt this required severing some less lofty heads. To disclaim me Robert vilified my work in an issue of *Poetry (Chicago)*, published "An Owl is an Only Bird of Poetry" subtitled "A Vale for James Broughton," and mocked me as

Mr. Fairspeech in a Dunciad against my theater work.

I am not that easily disposed of when my heartstrings have been attached to another's. I cherished Duncan's manic glees and greedy energy of mind. Together we had explored philosophies and prosodies, together we had hunted mushrooms and swum in the Pacific surf. Despite dismissal I held on to the long ties of kinship. Gradually he retied them. When he agreed to be my son's godfather in 1966 he wrote a shining ode for his christening. And in late 1973 on the occasion of my sixtieth birthday gala, in the Fine Arts Theater at the College of Marin, Duncan came onto the stage wearing a bear mask and a hairy gown, growling and swaying as he walked. Then, revealing his face, he read the following poem which testified to our long companionship as magickers of dark and light. I copy the original manuscript of this unpublished poem:

> I left my Shadow on the threshold
> of the New Age. Now going back to
> the Frontier I find he-she was all Light.
> In what a sun-dazzle that shining moves.
> I was the Dark One. As my Other moved on,
> I turned back to the Old Sun.
> Lingering among the young, I am
> a shadow fading in the light,
> deepening toward night, how often
> entirely going over to the dark surround.
> Powerful, powerful
> my spirit touches deep to sound.
> And it is all right as it goes.
> I am left right where I ought
> to be one. One with you then O
> friend in Time. Fellow thee,
> my companion thresholder.
>
> > (A Pre Preface for James on his
> > Sixtieth Birthday 10 Nov. 1973)

In later life Robert considered himself something of an oracle and dominated every gathering he attended. He would exhort, extol, and excoriate to awesome lengths. Jonathan Williams said Duncan could outtalk Buckminster Fuller and the Wicked Witch of the West put together. One remembers Marianne Moore's caution: "Blessed is the artist who knows that egomania is not a duty."

Duncan's loyalties could be as vehement as his prejudices. Once while I was driving Randall Jarrell back to his hotel after his reading at the Poetry Center Jarrell snickeringly remarked that Edith Sitwell's verse was as dessicated as her pussy. Duncan, who was riding with us, shouted to me: "Stop the car! I will not ride another mile with this despicable person!" He was adamant. I had to let him out at the next corner.

The last time I saw Duncan, a short time before he died, Robert Glück was pushing his wheelchair into the auditorium at San Francisco State where Ruth Witt-Diamant's friends were gathering for her memorial service. When I expressed compassion for his failing health, Duncan sneered angrily: "I suppose *you* will live to be ninety!"

Another influential postwar poet was William Everson. His thundering spiritual rage became even more impressive when he put on Dominican robes and called himself Brother Antoninus. Though he came from the farmlands of the San Joaquin valley, as did both Duncan and I, Everson wore the mien of a distressed Byzantine saint. On a visit to Mount Athos in 1985 I encountered several Greek orthodox monks whose agonized longing to be accepted by God reminded me of Brother Antoninus. Bill seemed always to be preparing for a crucifixion or recovering from one. His confessional performances often proved as painful for his audience as they did for him.

Beyond his vigorous verbal style Everson set another example for the poets of the region: he hand-printed his poems on his own press. This he did with an assertive skill that matched his verse. He set a tantalizing goal. Every poet in the region wanted to get his hands on a printing press.

Everson had developed his press skills during his years at the conscientious objector camp in Waldport, Oregon. There at what was called the Untide Press two of his disciples were Adrian Wilson and Kermit Sheets. By 1947 all three had come to live near one another in San Francisco. I became very fond of tall clarinet-playing Adrian. In the autumn of that year when he decided to choose fine press work as a career, he proposed to me the printing of a sheaf of my poems for Christmastime.

This became an Opus One for both of us. It comprised a dozen of my verses about the anxieties of childhood, each printed on a separate sheet of a different colored construction paper and embellished with an antique woodcut. In the chilly evenings of early December, ever cheerful Adrian printed the poems on a borrowed handpress stored in a potting shed behind a dilapidated mansion on O'Farrell Street. We collated the separate sheets and inserted them unbound into cardboard folders hand-colored by nursery school children. I called the collection *Songs for Certain Children.* We printed only seventy-five copies and we gave all of them to friends. Hence this item has become the rarest in my bibliography.

During this time I had also been involved in an experimental film project for the Art in Cinema program at the San Francisco Museum of Art. Hoping to pursue this enthusiasm, I had moved from Sausalito to an upstairs flat on Baker Street in the city. The landlords were three unmarried O'Leary sisters who charged me twenty-three dollars a month. The previous occupant, a ceramist friend, had painted the parlor indigo, the bedroom orchid, the dining room a gray violet he called "elephant's breath." The purple bathroom had a zinc tub, the pink kitchen an icebox awaiting weekly visits of a husky iceman.

Not sure what I should be doing there I consulted a novice psychoanalyst. When one has no lover to go to one goes to a shrink. He wasn't much help. He insisted that I was performing my Oedipus complex all wrong because I wanted to kill my mother and marry my father. He suggested I practice traditional fucking and take vitamin B. I abandoned him when I learned that he had drowned his brother.

Pauline Kael had offered to help me get settled in the flat. She was selling art books in Brentano's to pay rent on a furnished room in an alley. Acknowledging our mutual aloneness I offered her my more domestic haven and took comfort from her cooking, cleaning, and cuddling. She curtained windows with sheeting, upholstered Victorian sidechairs with tapa cloth a soldier had brought me from Hawaii, sewed stripes of Purple Heart ribbon from Army Surplus onto an old piano stool. My mother's baby grand was the one substantial furnishing.

But why was Pauline doing this when she disapproved of my life, my friends, and my writing? Her witty movie talk may have brought us together in the first place but it couldn't keep us there. We seldom agreed about movies we saw, and a critic in the house tends to intimidate spontaneity. Though I tried to engage her collaboration she never felt at ease with experimental cinema. She deplored little theater, little magazines, little films. She valued the big time, the big number, the big screen.

Then one day in the Brentano's store Pauline introduced me to Kermit Sheets, who was in atlases and reprints. This was both a momentous and an ironic meeting: momentous because Kermit became my partner in adventure for the next eight years, ironic because he shortly replaced Pauline as my roommate. I recognized at once that Kermit was a soul brother. Not merely because we were the same height and age and both natives of the San Joaquin (he from Fresno) but because we were harmonious opposites. We had similar passions for theater, poetry, and cinema, but unlike me Kermit was forthright, down-to-earth, modest, capable, factual, compassionate, and fiercely loyal. He was also physically stronger and had a happier relationship to realities.

When we met he and other refugees from Waldport were forming a new theater group called The Interplayers. He invited me to attend a rehearsal of a double bill he was preparing: *Aria da Capo* by Edna St. Vincent Millay and *Don Perlimplin* by García Lorca. I went that very evening. And the next evening, which was Saturday, I invited Kermit to drive down the coast to Half Moon Bay for an abalone dinner. We spent the night in a clapboard hotel above a bar. By morning we knew that we were fated to live and work together in affectionate harmony. I was sure I had Hermy to thank for this boon of a companion.

I took Kermit to the opening night of my play at Mills College. This satiric allegory in verse called *The Playground* had first appeared in *Theatre Arts* magazine in 1946. I had written the play in response to Hiroshima and the apprehensions that followed. It mocked people who bury their heads in the sand when the fate of the planet is at stake. At Mills College, however, Arch Lauterer produced it as a hippety-hop dance drama that eliminated most of my text.

This distressed Kermit even more than it did me, for he admired the script and hoped to produce it someday. While he was helping me with some revisions of the text, he suddenly exclaimed, "This wonderful work should be in book form!" Then after a moment added, "I could print it. Why don't we get a press and do it ourselves?" It took me only a moment to reply, "Why not?" Thus began the adventure of the Centaur Press, which we operated for five years.

Everson encouraged us to acquire a clam-action letterpress. The bargain one that Kermit located was a temperamental monster which outfoxed us until we learned how to respect its idiosyncrasies. We installed it in the basement of the building on Baker Street. For this we paid an extra $5 a month. At Everson's suggestion we bought a font of the handsome typeface called Centaur designed by Bruce Rogers. Since this was our only font, it seemed apt to adopt a centaur for our logo. We intended to print volumes by all our poet friends, but mine of course was to be the first.

I learned to set type, and to throw it, while Kermit sweated over the make-ready and inking. Luckily Adrian Wilson lived in the flat above our basement press room: he could be called down to disentangle a snafu. Ever since that first volume I have most cherished the books I have had a hand in physically shaping.

When *The Playground* came back from the bindery we invited everyone we knew to a publication party. Our narrow flat was so crowded that John Cage and Merce Cunningham never made it up the stairs. Elsewhere the book was ignored, but we sold enough copies that first night to cover the costs of the edition. At thirty-five I was euphoric over my first literary offspring. At thirty-five Whitman published *Leaves of Grass*, Mozart wrote *The Magic Flute*, Byron finished *Don Juan*, Buddha was enlightened, and I held in my hand a verse play of thirty-five pages.

Kermit's production of *The Playground* at The Interplayers ran for months. In the meantime we were at work on our second Centaur title, Robert Duncan's *Medieval Scenes*. That was followed by Madeline Gleason's *The Metaphysical Needle*. Next came *Orpheus* by Muriel Rukeyser. At that time Muriel was living near us in San Francisco arranging to be inseminated. Muriel was the first but not the last lesbian of my acquaintance who wanted to be a mother. I never learned whether anything came of it.

I did not learn till several years later why Pauline had practiced nest-making in my flat. After she moved to Santa Barbara she gave birth to a daughter whom she named Gina James. By the time I met this handsome child for the first time Pauline had married a man who owned twin repertory cinemas in Berkeley where she selected and annotated the programs. Her critiques on the local radio station formed the basis of her first book, *I Lost It at the Movies*. Becoming arbiter of filmic taste in Berkeley enhanced her sassy tone and her talent for contempt. When her audience disliked a mainstream movie she championed, she scoffed, "What else can you expect from a city where Dylan Thomas is a best seller?"

Another potent lady, though of a different stripe, had come to stay in San Francisco. Where Pauline was a brazen Artemis with hot arrows, Anaïs Nin was a would-be Circe always on the lookout for males to lure. More a queen bee than a devouring spider, she collected beautiful young men for her drones. She required them to be unconditional admirers of herself and her writings.

Anaïs felt sympathetic toward our Centaur Press since she had published her own books in Greenwich Village. Because her printer-lover Gonzalo in New York had become incorrigibly alcoholic and indifferent sexually, Anaïs gave us the font of sans-serif type that he had used to print her *House of Incest*. She encouraged me to set my own poems in type, saying, "Every writer should feel the weight of a word in his hand." Setting by hand each letter of my own words taught me forever after to retain in any line only what was essential.

Anaïs also offered us distribution rights to her unsold copies of *House of Incest*. She gave breathy readings from that book in our press room and became for a time our svelte good fairy, lending a perfumed tone to our inky basement. She found Kermit and me so sympathetic that she offered us the carved and inlaid Moroccan headboard which, she said, had graced the bed of her houseboat on the Seine where she and Gonzalo made love. This was the most impressive object in our thrift-store flat.

Anaïs had a much bulkier possession: her Diaries, those famous notebooks to which she had confided for many years her secrets and her fantasies. Lauded loudly by Henry Miller as the greatest literary work of the century but unseen by anyone else, the Diaries had acquired an ambiguous glamour. Anaïs stored these volumes in a bank of whatever city she was living in. They were her investment in her immortality. She visited them regularly in the vault of the Bank of America in San Francisco.

I asked her if we might print Volume One of the Diaries at the Centaur Press. At first she said "No," then coyly, "Maybe," then, "I'll get it out of the bank and look at it to decide."

Anaïs lived in such a network of impulsive deceptions that one never knew whether to believe her. She enjoyed appearing to be an impoverished free agent even though she was supported by her stockbroker husband Hugh Guiler in New York whose artistic pseudonym was Ian Hugo. When she wrote to Henry Miller in Big Sur that she was solitary and scrimping in San Francisco she was actually living in a fancy apartment on Buena Vista Heights where she showed me into her mirrored bedroom and struck enticing poses.

Also for the first time in her life Anaïs was driving a car. Or pretending to. Like everything else she did, she approached this activity intuitively. In this case she did not bother to learn how to shift the gears. She simply relied on the horn. Once I had a hair-raising ride with her across the city's hills and declivities during which she stopped for nothing: not red light, not through traffic, not fire engine. We managed to arrive undamaged, but I had no wish to repeat the experience.

Hugo arrived in San Francisco to join Anaïs and to join the Art in Cinema movement. He had acquired expensive camera equipment on which to learn filmmaking and he sought my collaboration. Wanting to enjoy a holiday while filming he invited me to accompany him to Mexico. There we traveled extensively and photographed randomly. In time we reached Acapulco where Anaïs awaited us.

In those days Acapulco was a fishing port with few hotels and unspoiled beaches. Hugo installed the three of us in the El Mirador where on the first morning as I got out of bed I stepped on a scorpion. Each day Hugo took me into nearby jungles where I helped him film swamps and birds and natives in hammocks which eventually he shaped into his first completed picture, *Ai-Ye*. We also shot scenes of Anaïs rocking in a hammock underwater for a fanciful portrait of her called *Bells of Atlantis*. On the soundtrack of this film she utters the reassuring line: "I always rise after a crucifixion." Evenings at the hotel, as we sat watching the young divers plunge into the sea from the perilous cliffs, Anaïs would ask Hugo to proposition any young man in the bar who caught her fancy. Being the most generous cuckold I have ever known, Hugo did her bidding without protest and withdrew into the background of her flirtations. He truly adored her. In her published Diaries, however, Anaïs ignored his existence. Publicly she played the role of indigent liberated woman artist who lived only for love. She enjoyed it both ways: her meal ticket and her romances. Her last major love object was Frank Lloyd Wright's grandson who lived in Los Angeles. She flew between Hugo in New York and Rupert in Silver Lake, calling this her "secret transcontinental bigamy." With a conspiratorial straight face Anaïs cautioned me, "Neither of them must ever know about the other." But she herself told everybody else.

While in Mexico City I had sought out Leonora Carrington at the behest of Wolfgang Paalen. She gave me the manuscript of a novel as mysterious as her surrealist paintings. Challenged by this superior competition Anaïs changed her tune. After altering the date of her birth she offered us Diary Number One for publication, proposing that we acquire subscribers to pledge $25 to pay for a fancy numbered edition. Phantoms of publishing glory tempted Kermit and me for a month until we realized that to print novels and extended confessions on our handpress would defeat the reason we had launched Centaur in the first place. So despite our polite regrets, the Diary went back into the bank, Leonora's novel returned to Mexico, and movers came to reclaim the Moroccan headboard. With some relief we started setting type for my collection of poems, *Musical Chairs*.

Anaïs always expected too much of her courtiers. Discovering their "shallowness" she would dismiss them with tragic wistfulness. I was one of her many disappointments. As she did to Gore Vidal and to others who "disappointed" her, Anaïs removed me from the published version of Volume Five except to include me on a list of mother-dominated homosexuals.

I did not see her for many years. Not long before her death a gala in her honor was mounted in the Pauley Ballroom on the Berkeley campus. Anaïs sat enthroned on the stage, flanked by minions and admirers. When I went up and knelt at her feet (since there was no other way to approach her) she exclaimed, "Oh James, I didn't think you still cared!"

Mother and son, 1915   Father and son, 1918

With grandparents, J.R. and Jennie. Modesto, 1916

San Rafael, 1932

L to R: James Broughton, Madeline Gleason, Robert Duncan
San Francisco, 1949

Filming *The Pleasure Garden*. London, 1952

J.B. filming *Mother's Day*. San Francisco, 1948

With Kermit Sheets, 1951

Café Tournon. Paris, 1954

Jess, J.B., Robert Duncan, Madeline Gleason, Helen Adam, and
Eve Triem, 1958

With Stan Brakhage, 1961

With Jonas Mekas and P. Adams Sitney. New York, 1974

The family. San Anselmo, 1974

Alan Watts, 1972

With Joel Singer, 1976

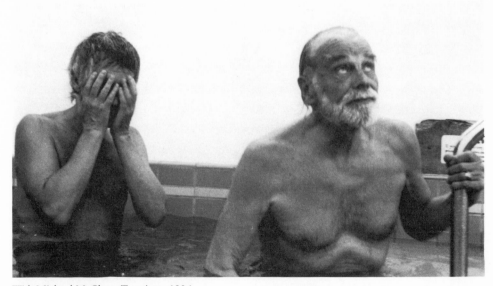

With Michael McClure. Tassajara, 1986

6

SCREENS TO HANG MIRRORS ON

IN THE wonderland of silent movies my childhood discovered its most sensory home. I could hear the slapstick disasters, smell the saddles of cowboys, taste every pie in the face, feel the paws of Rin Tin Tin. And where else could one behold Douglas Fairbanks on a flying carpet, Buster Keaton on a runaway locomotive, Lillian Gish on a runaway ice floe, Laura LaPlante being severed by a buzzsaw? How I longed to climb into that more vivid world.

It was not until 1945 when I returned to San Francisco that I met the man who would take me through the looking glass of the silver screen. Sidney Peterson was a tall and wryly charming litterateur with an educated eye and a discursive intellect. Our mutual delight in the comic quickened our acquaintance. Having admired my *Summer Fury* production Peterson proposed that he and I collaborate on his idea for a play based on the last years of Tolstoy's turbulent domestic life. He suggested that we transfer Yosnaya Polyana to a ranch in Sonoma Valley and model the protagonist on John Sutter.

When after weeks of convivial debate our plot got hopelessly tangled, the prospect of any feasible drama floated out the window. And out the window the sun was shining. At that point Peterson surprised me: "Why don't we get outdoors and make a movie instead?" So much for Tolstoy in California.

Now Peterson proposed that we attempt an experimental film in the manner of *Un Chien Andalou* by Dali and Buñuel. He knew only a little more than I did about actual moviemaking, so our lark got off to a blithe start. Using a borrowed 16 millimeter camera with black-and-white film we amused ourselves in a cemetery that was having its corpses removed so it could become a shopping mall. In order to have something live to shoot in the cemetery we also borrowed an aging actress and a pimpled adolescent.

Since Peterson operated the camera while I put things in front of it for him, his peculiar vision dominated the images. When we set up a mock brothel in an empty house I costumed the whores and manipulated the distorting mirror. Otherwise not much of me got into the film, except for parts of my anatomy. When my whole body does appear it has no head.

Edited and titled by Peterson, *The Potted Psalm* premiered at the San Francisco Museum of Art on the last program of an Art in Cinema series organized by a young enthusiast named Frank Stauffacher. The film looked grubby and opaque alongside of Maya Deren's *Ritual in Transfigured Time* on the same program, but it brought us some tiny fame as West Coast film pioneers.

The experience left me impatient to have a camera of my own. Now that I had learned the language of cinema I longed to put something on the screen more in tune with my own aesthetic. For me, translucence is the greatest of mysteries and the greatest virtue in a work of art.

Remembering that he owned a camera, I sought out Frank Stauffacher at the Museum. As perceptive as he was personable, raven-haired Frank was on the rebound from a tall blonde named

Martha, hence was willing to spend evenings with me. One night I plied him with gin and asked him if he would lend me his Bolex. His reply: "Yes. I will lend it to you. But I will have to come along with it." This was greatly more than I had hoped. So began a long, intense, and affectionate collaboration.

During Frank's active duty in the signal corps on Guadalcanal his Bolex had been dropped, stepped on, and left out in the rain. Tropical warfare had worn off the indicators on the aperture and the focus ring. Its pressure plate bumped the image, it made strange groans, the parallax was unreliable. Unless it became part of your own body, the camera would not work. But when it did work, it made beautiful pictures.

After our first day of test shooting I knew that Frank, the camera and I could see eye to eye. The next weekend with Kermit's assistance I staged some scenes in an empty lot with well-dressed friends playing at children's games. Adults engaged in childish behavior had been the device I used for the political allegory of *The Playground*. At first I had considered using that play as a scenario but as soon as we began filming in the alleys and backyards of the city nostalgic memories seemed to walk right onto the set and evoke the bewilderments of my own growing up.

Soon I had to ask: how could I re-create the truth of my San Francisco childhood without the Severe Eminence of my mother at the center of it? To portray the mother I chose one of my most beautiful friends, a talented pastelist from Bakersfield, because she possessed the iconic placidity of a silent movie star. Marion Osborn Cunningham did not attempt to act, she was simply there. Her presence dominated the film, which is how it acquired the ironic title of *Mother's Day*.

An early sequence filmed with Marion we called at the time "the princess in the tower." This follows the screen title reading "Mother always said she could have had her pick," which derived from Olga's boast of her debutante desirability: "I had so many suitors, I could have had my pick." When I asked her why she picked my father, she frowned, "I was so innocent. I didn't know beans."

For Mother as a picky debutante we positioned Marion in a top floor window where she leaned out like Rapunzel to size up her suitors below. This sequence, proceeding by staccato cuts, established the formal style for the rest of the filming. To indicate time changes I wanted Marion to appear in a different costume as each suitor proffered her a gift. I especially wanted a supply of period hats for her to wear throughout the filming. My wish was granted by a classmate from Stanford, Myna Brunton Hughes, who had once acted Mrs. Dangle to my Mr. Dangle in a Palo Alto production of Sheridan's *The Critic*. Myna had an aunt named Mrs. Plymire on Grove Street who had saved her best hat from each year since 1910, neatly packed away in its original hatbox.

My professor friend Frank Fenton, who later became a president of San Francisco State University, offered his roomy Victorian house for our interior scenes. He had given over its basement rec room to Kenneth Anger who was reading *House of Incest* and brooding over what would become his first authentic film, *Fireworks*. Fenton also loaned us his ex-lover, an actor with a handsome profile.

Others who appeared in the film were friends of mine, of Kermit's, of Frank's, and sometimes a mere passerby. In the very first shot the man sitting in the lap of a sculpted goddess is Lee Mullican, the visionary Oklahoma painter who lived with Stauffacher. The older white-haired mother figure trying to lure a young man with champagne and ladyfingers had in fact lured a young nephew of Will Wood into service as her resident gigolo.

Mirrors proliferate in *Mother's Day*, testimony to my mother's lifelong love affair with her reflection. How often I had gone to her dressing table to plead for some indulgence while she would sit rearranging her hair or her hat and never look at me and then would dismiss me with, "Don't you do another thing to make me ashamed of you. I hope someday you'll amount to something I can be proud of."

Rather than film an autobiographical report of my own mother complex I visualized a mother-complexity of many boys and girls conspiring against the strictures of an impervious widowed goddess. After many scenes of their defiant pranks these grown children needed some climactic image of escape from the household tyranny of the Mother. I threw all the symbols out the window — mirrors and hats and balls — and let a boy and a girl elope into an outdoor freedom. The sly Puck of the piece gives the unlikely lovers a heart to sit on and throws his cap in the air. Mother is last seen alone in her mansion androgynously dressed in jodhpurs and cap, clutching her riding crop.

It took months to edit the footage into some inevitable coherence. Meanwhile Kermit and I printed and published. He staged plays and I gave readings. We went to gallery openings for the martinis and sandwiches, to the Black Cat bar to buy Lucky Strikes for fifteen cents and listen to José sing Madame Butterfly, to visit Minor White and marvel at the navels he was photographing, to Murphy's Hot Springs in Big Sur before it dressed itself up as Esalen, where we chatted in the tubs with Henry Miller, Emil White, and other local characters. Any extra money went into the making of books and films.

Mother's Day was premiered at the San Francisco Museum in the fall of 1948. A memorable response came from Ruth Witt-Diamant who announced without explanation: "This is the greatest thing since Pavlov's dogs." A second showing was at a PTA fundraising in Three Forks, Montana, where one mother fainted.

Though it later became what is called a classic, initially *Mother's Day* aroused minimal enthusiasm. With one exception. Howard Brubeck loved the film so much he wanted to compose a musical score for it. Brother of Dave Brubeck, Howard taught music with Darius Milhaud at Mills College. He had become my close friend when we collaborated on a performance piece for Anna Halprin. I had assumed that *Mother's Day* would be shown silent as were those of many other experimentalists. This was due not only to a lack of funds but to the scarcity of recording equipment. In 1947 tape recorders were not yet in general use. Though I told Howard that the cost of adding a sound track to *Mother's Day* was prohibitive, he kept right on composing. As he completed each section he would play it for me on the telephone. The sounds so enchanted me that I had to relent.

I was able to relent thanks to an unexpected windfall from New York City. I had written Mrs. Henry White Cannon that I had completed another work. Her generous response paid for the music of *Mother's Day* as well as for the longstanding lab debt. In addition I could acquire Frank Stauffacher's Battered Bolex for my own. He was buying a new one: he intended to marry a petite blonde dancer and immortalize her on film. But tragedy struck Frank, as it also did Marion Cunningham. The two most gentle and lovable persons connected with the project were both victims of inoperable brain tumors. In shock and in sorrow I could not help wondering: were they sacrificial victims? Was this some revenge of the Terrible Mother?

New York audiences have often been for me either problematic or disastrous. My lyric California cheerfulness seemed to irritate East Coast cynicism. A prime example was the premiere of *Mother's Day* at Cinema 16 in the spring of 1949. With high hopes of a little big-time recognition Kermit and I had traveled on the transcontinental situp train *The Challenger*, carrying the only existing print of *Mother's Day* plus a fresh copy of *The Playground* to show booksellers.

In New York Amos Vogel informed us that he had made an addition to the program that would guarantee a successful reception for my work. His reason: the Cinema 16 subscribers, though liberal and discerning, were not familiar with what Amos endearingly called "ex-spear-mental" films. To remedy this ignorance he had engaged Parker Tyler to present a short speech before my film. Though I had never met Parker Tyler I knew his reputation as a surrealist poet and as the author of several obscure books on cinema. I looked forward to an evening of some literate verve.

My hopes began to sink when we arrived at the hall for the screening: the Central Needle Trades auditorium on West 26th Street had the intimacy of a car barn in Siberia. A documentary of an African tribe on the first half of the program contained bare-breasted women and dusty cattle, but the sound was muffled and the throw from the 16 millemeter projector in the far balcony produced a small dim image.

After the intermission Amos made a pitch for new subscribers before introducing Parker Tyler as the authority who would explain what to look for in a film like mine. Parker took his place at a lectern on the left side of the stage. After slowly adjusting his glasses and clearing his throat, he began to read from a sheaf of papers. Alas, his drawling Mississippi monotone was nearly unintelligible. One thing I could make out: he was not talking about *Mother's Day*.

Instead he was reading a perversely detailed and complexly phrased history of avant-garde cinema beginning with *The Cabinet of Dr. Caligari*. Although he was difficult to hear and to comprehend the audience kept its patience for the first few minutes. But when it became evident that he had many pages of history still to read, isolated shouts broke out: "Louder! We can't hear you! Speak up!" When Parker ignored these interruptions, continuing to mumble his polysyllabic sentences, the mood grew uglier. It began with fidgeting and murmuring and contemptuous mutters until the resentment burst forth with cries of "Shut up! Sit down! We want the movie!" accompanied by boos and some stamping of feet. Despite the disturbance Parker droned sublimely on.

Suddenly in the midst of this hiatus, a woman from the audience strode angrily up onto the stage, and squarely facing the crowd, began to shout back at them: "Have you no respect? Be quiet and listen to this man! He has important things to say!"

"Oh yeah?" came a voice from the balcony, "Who the hell are you?" Who she was was Maya Deren, hair blazing back from her face, eyes afire with righteous fury. But she did not deign to declare her identity to the audience. "This man is an important critic. You are insulting the most articulate friend we film artists have. He is sharing his knowledge here to introduce a new art form . . ."

Though momentarily silenced by this scolding the anger of the audience soon revived with as much intensity as Maya's contempt for it: "Get off the stage! Sit down! We didn't come here for a lecture! We want the movie!" Never one to be daunted by audience hostility, Maya's tongue sharpened under fire. The more she vilified the crowd the more vituperation she got in return. She had become the focus of resentment, not Parker, who stood gaping at his lectern.

Into this contretemps a stocky gray-haired man, rumpled and frowning, hurried up onto the stage. Was he coming to remove Maya forcibly? Not at all. Loudly and profanely he began his own tirade against the audience.

"You pigs! How dare you insult the most important woman in the American avant-garde, the high priestess of American filmmaking, the greatest artist of our time . . ." He rambled on with increasing incoherence while Maya stepped to one side, flinging her long shawl over her shoulder, and cocking her head like a vindicated goddess.

The man defending her was, I later learned, Willard Maas. But his defense was only creating greater tumult in the hall. While he fulminated, the outcries now directed at him devolved into one persistent chant: "We want the movie! We want the movie!"

Amos Vogel finally took action to save the situation. While Maya and Willard were still on stage defying the mob, and Parker still waiting in mid-paragraph by his lectern, Amos turned off all the house lights and turned on my film.

Mother's Day might as well have been set before a firing squad. The screen image was faint, the sound thin, and given the leisurely irony of the work its immediate impression—even to me—was of some fragile and remote chamber music. It could in no way compete with the drama in the hall. As Maya and Willard and Parker stumbled awkwardly to their seats in the dark, the hostility that had been directed at the three speakers was now diverted toward the screen. And what was on the screen was neither assertive nor shocking enough to appease the anger.

As proof of any avant-garde pudding, *Mother's Day* was a soufflé that not only fell, but was trampled on. Within a few minutes the audience began to walk out. During the entire twenty-two minutes of the film's duration the noise of the exiting obliterated what was unreeling on the screen. Only a few diehards sat it out. When the lights finally came up Maya and Willard and Parker were nowhere in evidence. Amos was embroiled at the door placating irate subscribers. Kermit and I slunk out to 26th Street into a chilly wind.

I was stopped by a bright-eyed stranger who introduced herself as Rosalind Kossoff, adding, "I don't understand your film but it impressed me. I'd like to see what I can do with it." Heading a company that distributed French documentaries, Rosalind wasn't able to do much, but she remained loyal to my work. As for our Centaur book, the only person in New York Kermit could interest was Robert Wilson of the Phoenix Book Shop, who over the years continued to collect everything I published.

Maya Deren and Willard Maas, however, became earnest friends of mine. And of Parker Tyler I have one final special memory. On the opening program of the retrospective of my work that Willard Van Dyke arranged at the Museum of Modern Art in 1973 to celebrate my sixtieth birthday, I showed a first sketch of my then unfinished autobiographical film *Testament*. Following the showing Parker came up to me with a warm handshake and made me promise not to change a frame of the final cemetery sequence. "It is perfect," he said, "absolutely perfect!" Within a year Parker had gone to his own cemetery.

As for Maya Deren, she was supremely conscious of being the high priestess of the American avant-garde cinema. She was also its social arbiter and ritual initiator. I often called her "The mother of us all" which did not amuse her since she was firmly unmaternal. But any young filmmaker had to earn her stamp of approval or risk being banished. When I was summoned to my private audience with her on Morton Street I shivered all the way up the stairs. Maya possessed the stare of Medusa and a head of hair to go with it, flaring out behind her as though she stood in a perpetual gale. Her gaze could reduce a mere male to a cold sweat and her cross-questioning took the form of sexual challenge. I feared that if I did not measure up to her demand she would, like the Queen of the Amazons, castrate me and fling me to the sharks. It was no good trying to joke one's way out of this: Maya was not only a student of voodoo, she did not know what a sense of humor was. As a result her attempted seduction of me was much funnier than she realized. Nevertheless we became polite cohorts in the small world of experimental filmmaking.

The last time I saw her, Maya was passing through San Francisco en route to Havana. At dinner with me and Sidney Peterson she grew almost mellow, she even smiled, and the three of us vowed lasting devotion to one another. She even sent me an affectionate postcard of Morro Castle. But back in New York she was provoked into such a fierce voodoo rage that she died of a cerebral hemorrhage.

Unlike Maya, Willard Maas had an abrasive sense of humor even to the perpetration of elaborate practical jokes. His social energies were more titillating and more memorable than any of the films he made. He was, up to his surprising death, my passionately devoted friend.

Before we ever met I received in Paris a telegram from him praising *The Pleasure Garden* which he had seen at the 55th Street Playhouse in New York. Since the film had been a disaster there, I was delighted to learn that someone had been touched by it. And Willard was always fulsome in his praise of whatever he cherished.

In New York he showed me his own work in the Soho studio he called Gryphon Films. In one corner he and Ben Moore were finishing *The Mechanics of Love* while carrying on tempestuous lovers' quarrels. In another corner Willard's wife Marie Menken was trying to edit her own films. Events were even stormier at the penthouse in Brooklyn Heights where Willard and Marie quarreled and reveled through the night, every night. Their alcoholic marriage bouts became legendary in New York circles. Although Edward Albee has denied it, *Who's Afraid of Virginia Woolf?* was widely rumored to have been inspired by the combative home life of Willard and Marie. It amused Willard to keep the rumor alive.

Over the years I would receive phone calls in California when either Marie or Willard would wake me up to complain about the other. Example: Marie calling, "Willard has just thrown the furniture out the window." This might be at 2:45 in the morning Pacific time. My wife would sleepily ask me, "Who *are* these people?"

Willard enjoyed throwing large objects out of windows. In the summer of 1963 he invited me to the New York Writers' Conference he had organized at Wagner College on Staten Island where he was a professor of poetry. The gathering flourished in the rambunctious spirit of its organizer. Not only did Willard fill the water pitcher on the panelists' table with straight vodka, he kept those of us housed in the dormitory awake most of the night with his pranks. He tossed Kenneth Koch's mattress out the window and when Kenneth objected, Willard tossed out the springs as well. While Paul Goodman would try to fuck a new student every night, Willard would do everything possible to interrupt the coitus, using stink bombs, gongs, and false telegrams. He also put a snake in Gerard Malanga's bed. It was the liveliest writers' conference I have ever attended.

Willard was so devoted to Marie that only four days after her death he took to his bed and never got up again. They were a pair passionate, pugnacious, and doomed. They were also memorable film artists. In the same year of 1943 that Maya made her first film *Meshes of the Afternoon*, Willard and Marie produced theirs, *Geography of the Body*, with poet George Barker reciting a poem on the sound track. That celebration of the human body, accompanied by evocative poetry, inspired my own filmic exploration of the body's geography in 1975. *Erogeny* was my homage to these pioneer visionaries and their endearing craziness.

At the time I had believed *Mother's Day* would be the only film I would ever make, but when I took the Battered Bolex into my own hands I wanted to explore a more fluid form of cinema, using poems as shooting scripts. As far as I knew no one had ever done this before.

I wanted to see a cinema that would dance to words. I wanted to unite my two passions, poetry and dance, into something magical. I had always wanted to dance impossible dances. As a boy I would turn on the Victrola, shed my clothes, and dance dance dance. Till my mother came storming in. I didn't enjoy being sent to proper dancing school to push little girls about. I preferred to leap and spin. At her house my great-aunt Marion didn't mind my turning on her player piano and flying about as long as I didn't knock over her Louis Seize end tables. Or as long as alcoholic Uncle Henry didn't come in and squirt me with a seltzer bottle.

I decided to choose certain amorous poems from my yet unpublished *An Almanac for Amorists* and film vignettes of love-hungry daydreamers to illustrate them. This took the form of a dancing sonata: an allegro for a pubescent Game Little Gladys, a pastorale for a twenty-year-old Gardener's Son, a scherzo for a schitzy thirty-year-old Princess Printemps, and an adagio for an Aging Balletomane. This choreography for camera I called *Four in the Afternoon*, and used poems to voice the quandaries of each protagonist. Performers included dancers Anna Halprin and Welland Lathrop with members of their company, as well as actors from Kermit's theater.

Four in the Afternoon gratified another of my passions: statuary both sculpted and posed. Little Gladys trots down most of the outdoor staircases on Telegraph Hill till she comes to her dreaming place: the foundations for a yet unbuilt housing project. On these pedestals she conjures with her jump rope living statues of twelve ideal suitors.

The Gardener's Son hoses down replicas of classical goddesses in Sutro Gardens, still in those days an unmanicured remnant of a once private estate overlooking the Pacific. My Aunt Esto had first taken me there when I was a boy. That initial encounter with sculptures of the gods haunted my life for years and deeply affected all my work in cinema. No wonder I loved Renaissance Italy when I finally encountered it.

The pseudo-classical Palace of Fine Arts where Princess Printemps is pursued around massive pillars had been another of my childhood dream places. At the time of our filming the plaster of Paris was falling from the dome and the grounds were boarded up. I had to get entry permission from the Parks Department, who allowed me only one day's access.

By contrast, The Aging Balletomane in the untidy backyard of 1724 Baker Street conjures his living statue of a Swan Lake ballerina atop an old stool: "O in the days when we danced!"

Four in the Afternoon needed music with a light touch. Brubeck had moved to San Diego State so I called up Milhaud at Mills College. For years confined to a wheelchair, he said, "I don't need to see your movie, just send me the times." When I protested he countered: "Better you take a young composer to do it. I have many here. I will send you a good one."

That is how a serious young man with spectacles and a worried look turned up at my door: his name was Bill Smith, or more properly William O. Smith. I never learned what the "O" stood for. When I showed him the work print of the film he made neither notes nor comments, asking only when I would need the score.

When it came time to record the music I called up O. Smith to alert him. "That's okay," said he. "Should I hear the score first?" I asked. "Not necessary," he replied. The following week Smith arrived with four musicians, recorded a score in one take, and quietly departed. The music fit perfectly.

Another amorous poem that I wanted to visualize was "Loony Tom's Song."

Love so they tell me, love so I hear,
love waves the trumpet and butters the tree.

But love will come tooting only if free
And only to me.

La diddle la, the hydrant chatted.
Um titty um, the milkpail said.

Though it began as a brief scherzo in slapstick style, it skipped so far away with me that it became a film on its own, *Loony Tom, the Happy Lover*. Personifying a daft Chaplinesque Pan, Kermit capered across a sunlit countryside making love to everyone he encountered as well as prodding polite art-lovers into one another's arms. The style paid tribute to the impudence of Mack Sennett comedy while affirming the lyric abandon of Autolycus. To accelerate rhythm and exaggerate gesture the Bolex and I shot the film entirely in fast motion. Golden Gate Park provided the countryside and farm which amorous Tom skipped through. The ladies in the barnyard came from Kermit's theater, wearing costumes out of a Synge play, *The Well of the Saints*.

Another film grew out of the only poem of mine ever accepted by the *New Yorker*: "A Lad from the Cold Country."

When I dwelt in the wood in a wind-cracked hut,
(at a waterwheel pinch the rivers flow)
I seldom bothered the shutters to shut,
for the northern maids are the warmingest, O.

But when I came on to the company town
(at a waterwheel pinch the rivers flow)
I hastened to pull the shades all down,
for the midland maids are the harmingest, O.

But when I moved down to the shore of the sea
(at a waterwheel pinch the rivers flow)
I threw the doors open fancy and free,
for the southern maids are the charmingest, O.

Rather than a dancing poem this suggested a freewheeling narrative: an innocent country boy going to the big city in search of an ideal mate encounters temptations and frustrations along his bewildered way. Here I spoofed the classic adolescent adventure as well as making a joke of my own misguided efforts to grow up straight and square. Hence it seemed apropos that I enact the naive traveler myself while Kermit pushed the Bolex button. I called the film *Adventures of Jimmy* since Jimmy was the nickname I had discarded in my twenties. When I fled from Stanford I thereafter called myself James (as in Saint and King) hoping that would give my persona more maturity.

The form of *Adventures* derived from a forgotten French film of the thirties by Sascha Guitry called *Diary of a Scoundrel,* the tongue-in-cheek parable of a peripatetic rake. In the opening scene he is revealed as such a naughty boy that he is denied his supper. His entire glum family sits around a table munching mushrooms. When his voice-over says, "Alas, the mushrooms were poisonous," they abruptly disappear. In one cut he was freed of all his relatives. I used a similar narrative voice with my Candide's ten-minute quest for an ideal mate.

Filming involved a few accidents. While I was directing a pseudo-South Sea episode of saronged maidens floating on Sausalito Bay, a sudden gale came up and capsized their boat. The ladies managed to swim ashore but I fell off the pier into the bay and broke a rib.

The music for *Jimmy* was the gift of a beautiful friend: bright, curious, nervous Weldon Kees, poet, occasional painter and amateur musician. When Weldon saw the rough cut of *Jimmy* he laughed uncontrollably, saying it was the story of his own life. With a combo of musicians from the Art Institute he improvised a lively score built upon a theme he called "The Jimmy Waltz."

Often when Weldon visited us he would linger on, as if trying to stir enough courage to share some profound confidence. I did not suspect how profound the secret must have been. His abandoned car was found at the Golden Gate Bridge, but his body was never recovered. The mystery of poets' departures! Like Lew Welch, last seen hiking away from Gary Snyder's house into the Sierras. Does ascension offer a convenient exit for poets? One day in 1938 my own great-uncle Leonard Bates, a compulsive scribbler of verse, climbed to the top of Mount Atlas in Sonoma County and was never seen again.

In making the films after *Mother's Day* I went on the supposition that Mrs. Cannon would continue her support. I kept sending letters to her each time I completed a new work, but I received no replies other than a notice from the New York post office that she had moved to Cleveland. The lab bills were still unpaid a year later when Kermit and I were on our way to Britain. When I phoned Mrs. Cannon's family mansion in Cleveland Heights a servant informed me without explanation that the lady could not come to the phone. In desperation I took a taxi to her house. A maid opened the door, took my name and left me standing outside. She returned to announce: "Mrs. Cannon says she does not know who you are." Then added, shaking her head, "Mrs. Cannon no longer knows who anybody is."

7

THE OTHER SIDE OF THE SEA

IN AUGUST OF 1951 Kermit and I sailed for Southampton in the smallest inside cabin of the *Nieuw Amsterdam*. We were seeking a more sympathetic country. Not only had the Korean War increased military censorship, but the excesses of Senator McCarthy and his gross sidekick Roy Cohn had made liberal thought perilous.

More than once the FBI had come around to inquire about my poet friends. Because Philip Lamantia had applied for C.O. status they wanted to know whether he was a Communist. Though I scoffed at the accusation, they persisted: if Philip was a poet with no visible means of support he must be homosexual and all homosexuals were, of course, Communists.

Such absurdity had become intolerable and friends like Kenneth Anger and Robert Creeley had already taken refuge in Europe. We sublet our Baker Street flat to Robert Duncan and Jess, expecting to return within a year. Instead I stayed abroad four years. I must have suspected this possibility, for I had brought along my well-worn traveling companion, Emerson's *Essays*, as well as my Roget and my unabridged Webster 2nd edition that Kermit had given me for Christmas.

Happier causes than political disquiet lured us abroad. The most alluring was an invitation to appear for the showing of our films at the Edinburgh International Film Festival, at that time the most prestigious movie event in Britain. I had also been heartened by news that *Mother's Day* had been honored at an International Experimental Film Congress in Belgium. Furthermore it had been the subject of a term seminar at the University of Liège.

A subsequent invitation came from the British cartoonist Gerard Hoffnung to be guests at his home in London. I had met Hoffnung at the New York penthouse of Fleur Cowles when she gave a cock-tail party for contributors to her dressy literary magazine, *Flair*. On that occasion Hoffnung had asked me if I had any funny story he could illustrate for a book. When I sent him an expanded version of my narration for *Adventures of Jimmy*, retitled *The Right Playmate*, he was delighted and wanted me to collaborate with him when I came to London.

Hoffnung lived in a pseudo-Tudor cottage in Golders Green that could have been a model for the witch's house in *Hansel and Gretel*. An obese troll of a man, pinched into vests and stiff collars, he lived in bachelor clutter with his sullen German housekeeper. His tuba he often brought to the dinner table where he would shake the house with bursts of sonic farting that sent the housekeeper screaming into the kitchen. A contributor to *Punch* and proud of being an eccentric joker, he felt compelled to be funny at every moment of the day. Even when we carried *The Right Playmate* manuscript into the hushed and paneled publishing office of Rupert Hart-Davis, Hoffnung had to pull out a trick cigar. Kermit and I left soon for Scotland.

Despite its discomforts and peculiarities I had quickly fallen in love with England. It was after all the place of my Broughton roots, as well as the roots of my literature. Despite their odd meals and odder habits, the British fascinated me. They could be at once gracious and rude, stuffy and imaginative, silly and proper.

Our London liaison to the Edinburgh Festival was the British Film Institute in Shaftesbury Avenue. This government agency became our sheltering haven during the years we lived in Britain. The Institute's unfailingly gracious director, a Scot named Denis Forman, I immediately claimed for my pantheon of heroes. Along with Basil Wright and Paul Dehn, Denis had been on the selection committee for the festival when they screened *Mother's Day* and *Loony Tom* for the first time. These three gentlemen became our intimate friends as well as our long-suffering sponsors.

Basil Wright, who had made one of my favorite documentaries, *Song of Ceylon*, lived in Kensington with his parents and his young Malaysian companion named Kassim. Paul Dehn, poet and film critic for a daily paper, lived in a Chelsea dollhouse with his young musical companion named Jimmy who wrote scores for horror films. Denis Forman lived in Kent with his tall wife named Helen who looked even more statuesque after Denis received his knighthood and she became Lady Denis.

Denis took me to lunch at one of the hallowed mysteries of London: a traditional men's club. At another time he introduced me to a different English phenomenon, Stevie Smith. In an Edinburgh pub I met Hugh MacDiarmid in a kilt. And from Edinburgh one day Denis drove us to his family seat in the lowland countryside to have tea with his parents. His father marched up and down on the terrace talking to himself while his mother served us high tea wearing a formal hat. She said her cook had been so pleased that Yankees were coming she had made both baps and bannocks for us. After tea we were taken across the puddled farm to "see the pigs."

Edinburgh proved a gray and damp place for an arts festival. At the airport, as he eagerly boarded his return flight to Milan, an Italian journalist informed me that Scotland was an "aquarium for grouse." More intimidating to me than the weather was the statue of John Knox in the city wagging his no-no finger at earthly pleasures. No wonder the Scots brewed whisky: their prime solace for the curse of Calvinism. At the film festival's official luncheon given by the Lord Provost in City Chambers the waitresses kept refilling our glasses with straight Scotch whisky while we partook of an array of fish, flesh, and haggis. Sitting between film critic Dilys Powell and Swedish director Alf Sjoberg I soon found myself holding onto the table to keep from flopping into either of their laps.

The praise given my lyrical films from professional documentarians like John Grierson and Paul Rotha amazed me. Michael Powell, then basking in the success of *The Red Shoes*, interviewed me for the *New Statesman* while Gavin Lambert wrote an appreciation in *Sight and Sound* of which he was editor. At the London Film Club Lindsay Anderson arranged a showing for me and berated the audience: "What's the matter with this country? Isn't England supposed to be a nation of poets? Aren't we supposed to know how to make films? Why can't we make something like *Four in the Afternoon?*" At that moment I lost my heart permanently to Lindsay Anderson.

Lindsay lived with Gavin Lambert in a London mews. He was a testy, outspoken, lovable Scot while Gavin was a willowy, soft-spoken intellectual whose hair had a mind of its own. For many years these two were as intimately involved in our lives as they were in one another's. Lindsay would eventually direct *If* and *O Lucky Man*, but at this time he was committed to documenting working conditions in the Midlands. Gavin was happier when he got to Hollywood where he could write books like *Inside Daisy Clover* and hobnob with George Cukor and Christopher Isherwood.

In London I renewed my acquaintance with Dylan Thomas, pub crawling with him through Soho. He and I had become friends in California during his reading tours of the States. One weekend we had been together in Big Sur where Dylan, beer bottle in hand, on the terrace of Nepenthe delivered a thundering extempore ode to

the Pacific Ocean. If Jeffers taught me not to be afraid of consonants, it was Dylan who taught me to enjoy sibilants. I also relished
his impish wit ("Oh, isn't life a terrible thing, thank God?") as I was
equally awed by his incantatory vocal style.

In the London winter of 1952 I was astonished to observe
Dylan's agony at an ICA Gallery event. Before getting up to perform
his poetry that night he sat next to me trembling and sweating and
gulping till I thought he would become seriously ill. I was the one
who should have been shaking with stage fright for I was scheduled
to read right after him. Dylan had arranged my inclusion on the
program with himself and Vernon Watkins. To that audience I was a
nobody while Dylan's fame was widespread. Despite my eagerness
to make an impression at my London debut as a poet, a reeking
pea-soup fog slowly filled the hall and by the time I had finished
reading I could no longer see the audience. And they were busy
coughing.

Occasionally I was asked, "Why don't you make a film in
Britain?" When I sought Denis Forman's sponsorship for such a
project he explained that the Institute could not give money to foreign artists. But a week later he called to say that he and Basil and
Paul were willing to form an independent committee to solicit funds
for me to make a film in the spirit of *Loony Tom*. This generosity,
in a country financially strapped from the war and still under strict
rationing, made me forever devoted to England. They called their
committee Flights of Fancy.

After the glum indifference to my work in the USA the articulate
approval of Britain exhilarated me. Was this island kingdom my
rightful home? Added to its traditional charms were the pleasant
orgies at Peter Watson's house.

How to express my gratitude in filmic terms? Loony Tom had set
forth every morning to arouse madness of love in any stranger he
encountered. In what form could a similar spirit release desires
locked up on Shakespeare's sceptered isle? Taking a cue from Ariel I

began to visualize a satiric fable with fairy magic in it. Two encounters focused this vision.

When I attended a Christmas pantomime and fell in love with the plump actress playing an absent-minded fairy I went backstage to meet Hattie Jacques and asked her to be a fairy godmother in my film. Hattie replied: "When do we start?"

A place in which to act out foolish magic did not manifest until the day Mary Lee Settle and Douglas Newton took us out to suburban Sydenham to see the ruins of the Crystal Palace Gardens. The park had been closed to the public since 1937 when the great glass building had come crashing down in a fire. Its abandoned public gardens had been enclosed in such a high wall that it was necessary to climb a tree in order to behold the surprises it contained. Before me extended a dilapidated splendor ready-made for a flight of fancy: acres of dislodged statuary, fallen urns, lichened balustrades and great staircases going nowhere, the whole place overgrown and awry. As a setting it suggested nothing less than the debris of Western civilization.

When I learned that the Duke of Edinburgh headed a committee planning to level the Gardens into a community playing field I resolved to exploit this enchanted ruin before it disappeared forever. There Loony Tom could be reconstituted as a fairy godmother liberating the woeful and repressed. There I might reclaim the spirit of Puck and the bower of Titania in defiance of the puritan foes of joy. Did I already hear the opening line of the film that Hattie Jacques would speak: "Here one at a time come the curious strangers, seeking what pleasure they can, in a midsummer afternoon's daydream?"

That autumn of 1951 Kermit and I had lived on Baker Street sharing John Grierson's flat with Jim Beveridge of the National Film Board of Canada. But at the first of the year King George died and the black of mourning plunged London into pervasive gloom. We escaped to the continent, sat up in trains down into Italy, and in a pensione on Capri Kermit helped me write the script for what would be called *The Pleasure Garden*. Neither of us had ever written a screenplay.

To indicate the plot we devised I will quote from a synopsis I prepared for the press: A puritanical Minister of Public Behavior attempts to curtail the enjoyment of the lonely strangers who come to a grandly dilapidated public park where they act out their fantasies. He tries to arrest them and turn the park into a cemetery, but a fat fairy godmother comes to their rescue with impish tricks that spark a rebellion against prudery and launch a victory for the pleasures of love.

Returning to London in the spring we took rooms in the attic of Barbara Jones' house on the edge of the heath in Hampstead. She was at work on her book of odd English architectures, *Follies and Grottoes*. Barbara owned a folly of her own: a yellow vintage roadster which she did not know how to drive. When I persuaded her that it would make a splendid vehicle for a fairy godmother and she herself a photogenic chauffeur, she succeeded in running into more than one wall before we completed the sequence.

In our absence Flights of Fancy had gathered enough money for us to begin filming. Lindsay Anderson offered to be my producer if I would go all out and film in 35 millimeter. He engaged Walter Lassally as cameraman and lured actors from the professional theater, including Jill Bennett who was in a Pinter and Maxine Audley who was in a Shakespeare. Hattie Jacques brought her husband John Le Mesurier to play the Minister of Public Behavior, as well as two of her music hall cohorts, Diana Maddox and John Heawood. Kermit played the traveling cowboy, Skipalong Sam.

Denis Forman persuaded the London County Council to let us use the Crystal Palace grounds. When I confided my intention to shoot the entire film in the open gardens during the month of July, Denis taunted me: "Dear boy, this is not California. Don't you know that it rains all summer?" But Hermy must have worked overtime in the North Sea cloudbank, for that year England experienced a severe drought. Rain did not fall until the coronation day of Elizabeth II.

Under the benevolent skies I devised the actions with the cooperation of a jovial crew who donated their talents and time. Since my committee had raised only a few hundred pounds the film had to be made with all the love it could get. Sir Michael Balcon of Ealing Films loaned us handcuffs, a hearse, a rifle, and a bass fiddle, while aptly enough members of the British Board of Censors portrayed the official spoilsports. Of all the scenes I invented on the spot I was most pleased with the finale when the fairy's magic stole becomes the object of a tug-of-war between black-coated gravediggers and lightly dressed lovers. This transforms her disguise as a fortune teller into a tutued and tiaraed fairy queen supplied with a barrage of spellbinding bubbles.

After we had been filming for a month, a courier from the Institute came jogging onto the set crying, "Stop! You must stop at once! There is no money left!" Despite gaps in the continuity, production had to halt. Flights of Fancy was not only broke, it was in debt. Kermit and I went to a lake in the Alps and rowed about moodily for a week.

Thanks again to Denis Forman an inactive government unit called Colonial Films loaned us drafty editing space in a back room where we studied our footage on a movieola and made a roughcut. The committee seemed to like what they saw and vowed to solicit more funds.

I had planned on postrecorded dialogue, plus a musical score with songs. I needed a composer who would set my verses and write forty minutes of music continuity for no fee. I got nowhere until Dylan Thomas brought John Davenport into my life. A book critic and art world busybody, Davenport suggested another drinking crony, the neo-classic composer Stanley Bate. Since I had once heard Sir Thomas Beecham conduct a likable suite by Stanley I agreed to show him the script. Despite being drunk whenever we conferred, as well as itchy and morose, small-boned Stanley composed in a month's time spry settings of my verses, plus a graceful score à la Poulenc for a harpsichord quintet. I could not imagine how he did it. He often appeared black and blue from beatings by his husky Brazilian wife. Only a year later he died in his bathtub.

To compose the texts of the songs I had gone to Dublin for a week where I loitered along the Liffey and its riverside pubs, eavesdropping on Irish speech. This greatly enhanced the lilt of my lyrics such as,

Strangers we are, the world and I,
curious strangers passing by.
My heart is locked up like a wishbone dry,
the world's pretty strangers touch and go by.

One morning I heard myself singing a tune for the love-seeking cowboy. Had the long-ago lap of my Uncle Jim in the Mother Lode inspired this American bounce?

I've come all the way away
from Californ-i-ay
alookin for a gal as sweet as Mom.
I like all the gals I've met
but I haven't met her yet,
the one who'll be as sweet on me as Mom.

With a slightly pained expression Stanley agreed to incorporate my frontier tune into his score.

Meanwhile Flights of Fancy had struck a blank wall. When their most promising backers, two well-moneyed celebrities, had viewed the silent roughcut Terence Rattigan guffawed loudly while Anthony Asquith shed one small tear. Neither offered a shilling. With no funds to pay for sound recording or completing the film, plus a debt which now reached a thousand pounds, Dennis was forced to inform me, "We're very sorry, James," said Denis. "It was a good try but we have done all we can. We still believe in you even if you can't finish your film."

On my knees in Westminster Abbey I invoked the advice of Hermy. I asked him how I could get rid of my ulcer and where could I borrow $3,500 for the outstanding debt, and somehow raise more to complete the sound track and printing. He reminded me that whenever I consulted the *I Ching* for advice I invariably drew "Perseverance furthers." Then he went to work and without any lo and behold, a real life fairy godmother manifested in the person of Basil's doting mum Gladys Wright. Despite my stepping on her train at the premiere of Britten's *Gloriana* at Covent Garden she donated enough to keep creditors at bay and get the film through recording and editing. We worked at panic haste in order to have a release print ready for the film's premiere at the Curzon Theater.

At the press preview Kenneth Tynan sat up front conspicuously reading a copy of *Il Corriere di Milano*, Stephen Spender said to me, "Don't you think your film is rather too pleasant?" while Roger Manville frowned, "James, when will you get over your obsession with sex?" Nevertheless my supporters rallied. Gavin Lambert persuaded William Whitebait to write sweet praise for *Sight and Sound* while Denis Forman persuaded the French officials to accept *The Pleasure Garden* as an official entry from England to the Cannes Festival the following May.

By the time of that festival in 1954 I had been living alone in Paris for most of the winter. Kermit had sailed home on a freighter from Antwerp, anxious to work again in his theater. I had remained to circulate in expatriate circles. Along with my official invitation to Cannes came a ticket on *Le Train Bleu* and a week's lodging at *Le Grand Hotel*. I enjoyed the sleeping car on the famous express to the Riviera that had carried international spies and dubious contessas in the fictions of E. Phillip Oppenheim and Maurice Dekobra. A young archaeologist from Nashville, who lived next door to me in my Paris hotel, had loaned me his tuxedo and the necessary trappings.

Among the posturing starlets and bustling agents at the Carlton Hotel I discovered Ian Hugo. Despite an aching back he accompanied me to my premiere in the Palais du Cinema. For the occasion *The Pleasure Garden* boasted French subtitles that Jacques Brunius and I had devised. During most of its projection the late arriving black-tie audience noisily tried to find seats in the dark, chattering as they settled themselves. Since *The Pleasure Garden* preceded a feature film from Egypt, I was assigned to a box with the official Egyptian delegation who did not arrive until my film had ended. And it had ended to the faintest smatter of applause. Despite Hugo patting me politely on the shoulder, I sensed fiasco in the air. The Egyptian film did not help. It ploddingly pursued the antics of a spoiled heiress with a tennis racket who drove around Alexandria in a convertible running over her lovers. It had little to do with Egypt and even less to do with the art of cinema.

No one spoke to me in the lobby. Hugo hobbled back to the Carlton and I took my sense of failure to the bar. Hence I was amazed a week later when I received word that *The Pleasure Garden* had won an official festival prize. I presumed that Cocteau, chairman of the jury, had proposed this honor. But the jury member who had insisted on honoring my film proved to be a petite pixie-eyed film director from Denmark named Astrid Henning-Jensen. She told me that once she had persuaded him to create a special category, Cocteau had chosen the designation of my award: *prix de fantaisie poètique.*

When he bestowed the prize Cocteau kissed me on both cheeks, saying, "Bravo! An American who made a French film in England" and remarked how much my comic fantasy owed to the cinema of Clair and Vigo. I told him that I had seen *Beauty and the Beast* three times before making *Mother's Day.* He could not know that I had always been partial to the arts of France: loved Rabelais more than Goethe, Ravel more than Tchaikovsky and Matisse more than

Rembrandt. To prolong the glow of being praised in France by a French artist whom I revered I tried to hold Cocteau's attention. My gleeful manner seemed to ruffle him. He fired off a battery of aesthetic chatter and then abruptly slipped away. At that moment I realized that Cocteau's gifts did not include a sense of humor. He was basically as romantic as Wagner.

To keep my spirits bubbling I ordered a bottle of Mumm's to share with my hostess Mme. Germaine Picabia whose houseguest I had been during the final festival week. She had housed me in a room whose walls reached to the ceiling with Picabia canvases.

Through the years I renewed my acquaintance with adorable Astrid Henning-Jensen. As recently as 1988 I relished her wit at the Hans Christian Andersen Film Festival in Ødense to which Jorgen Roos had invited me to be a member of the jury. Denmark had responded more heartily to *The Pleasure Garden* than any other country. The Danes could easily approve of a fairy-operated society that relished mischief and kisses more than rules and scoldings.

On my first visit to Copenhagen in 1952 I had been smitten by Jorgen's witty charm and his blond aura so reminiscent of Emil and of Littlejohn. When in the autumn of 1954 I was invited there again by the Danish Film Institute, I accepted eagerly. But Jorgen had left on a film expedition to Greenland.

At the Institute then my host was Ove Brusendorf, an expansive sybarite and collector of erotica. He housed me in an historic manor where I occupied a long seventeenth-century drawing room with a canopied bed at one end and a painted porcelain stove at the other. A turbaned cook as roly-poly as Mrs. Jack Sprat brought me hearty breakfasts of ham and cheese and eggs and pastry and sometimes herring. Brusendorf also provided me with a sturdy location scout whose hips I held onto as he sped me around the countryside on his Lambretta to show me unusual playground sites. But soon I recognized the folly of such a quest. No matter how lovable I found the Danes, why should I expect them to finance another version of "curious strangers passing by?" Furthermore despite the prize from Cannes *The Pleasure Garden* had not met with much approval.

In New York it was hooted off the screen at the 55th Street Playhouse. People demanded their money back, the theater yanked the film, and the editor of *Films in Review*, Mr. Henry Hart, denounced it as "a film of psychopathological befuddlement, hostility, hatred and despair." This scarcely encouraged me to return to the United States. Nor was recognition at Cannes awarding me vistas of fresh opportunity. The only straw that blew my way: a London producer inquired whether I would prepare a screen treatment of Max Beerbohm's *Zuleika Dobson*. With difficulty I got halfway through the book. My own poetic visions aroused no interest in the prose minds of the movie business. Once again the poet in me rebelled against struggling upstream in a mainstream industry. Years later Pauline Kael told me that this decision was the greatest mistake of my life.

I went back to Paris where I could feel more like a poet. Paris is where in 1953 I celebrated my fortieth birthday at a feast with writer friends and wondered whether I would ever write anything profound. Paris is where I learned to prefer wine to gin and to appreciate the importance of sauces. Paris is where I met Brancusi and Ned Rorem, Genet and Genêt, and Giacometti. Paris is where I left violets on the doorstep of 11 rue de Fleurus and a green carnation in Père Lachaise. Paris is where I met Alice B. at the opening night of *Four Saints in Three Acts* wearing a hat the size of a parasol and where Mary Meerson, the mistress of Henri Langlois of the Cinemathèque, assured me that she was the reincarnation of Oscar Wilde. Paris is where I experienced three memorable events: *Les Indes Galantes* of Rameau at the Opera, Colette's funeral, and James Leo Herlihy on a corner of the Place de l'Odeon one afternoon in September. On that occasion Herlihy walked away from my praise of his beauty. Not until thirty years later in Los Angeles did he acknowledge that we were soul brothers.

Edouard Roditi introduced me to French intellectuals on the right bank. Eugene Walter introduced me to American expatriates on the left bank. Eugene insisted that I move into his hotel, the Helvetia, on the rue de Tournon near the Senat and the Luxembourg Gardens. The Helvetia was a narrow hotel operated by a sober Breton and his effusive wife from Bayonne. It boasted one trickle of a shower on the second floor, toilet paper scissored from the tabloid *l'Express*, and indulgent house rules. "Only the enlightened live here," said Eugene.

One of those was Jean Garrigue who had strung a clothesline across her room for her many finches. Stanley Kunitz followed Jean around the quarter even though she was still faithful to Josephine Herbst. I enjoyed my top-floor front room with its view of the ugly bell tower of St. Sulpice. Looking over *les toits de Paris* I recalled Satie and Picabia dancing in slow motion on the roof of *Entr'acte*.

In the room next to mine my friend Zev broiled scampi in his fireplace and tossed salad in his bidet. In Centaur Press days Zev had embellished my *Playground* book with his deft and daft drawings. When the city of Monterey condemned his Crazy Crescent, the fantastic collaged house he had built with his own hands, he forsook California and came to join me in Europe carrying only a turkey roaster for his suitcase. He and I traveled in Sweden and Morocco and shared a house in Torremolinos for a winter, but once he arrived in Rome Zev stayed there the rest of his life. In his Trastevere apartment he created delicious canvases and sumptuous meals. I once watched him eat an entire coconut layer cake for breakfast. Did his passion for food contribute to his death in a Rome hospital in 1985? By the time his widow arrived from California his paintings and possessions had been whisked away by his lover, an unscrupulous carpenter from Ostia.

Across the street from the Hotel Helvetia the Café Tournon was at that time a major hangout for literary Americans living in Paris. Along the sidewalk they sat and gossiped and flirted and chewed intellectual fat from morning *café au lait* to lunchtime *paté* sandwiches to *bière* and Perrier at night. The place had an impervious waiter and several pinball machines. When empty it was a room of drab walls, splintered chairs, and smoky noise. Only the tables out front invited lingering. Yet Evan Connell sat a whole winter against the rear wall writing *Mrs. Bridge*, his long hair and drooping mustache making him look like Robert Louis Stevenson.

Around the corner in a tiny office in the rue de Fourney the *Paris Review* was in the process of getting born. This brought George Plimpton and Bob Silvers and sometimes Peter Matthieson to huddle at a sidewalk table. At another table the boys from *Merlin*, Alexander Trocchi and Austryn Wainhouse, debated Beckett and de Sade with Christopher Logue. *Native Son* novelist Richard Wright lived around the other corner in the rue de Condé with Ellen, his white New Yorker wife. Younger Ralph Ellison often turned up as did James Baldwin, though they did not live in the neighborhood. White novelists included Max Steele and the unforgettable *enfant terrible*, Alfred Chester, he of the hairless face and ratty toupee, who lived in a tiny room in Montmartre with an Israeli pianist named Arthur and a moth-eaten dog named Pettro. Alfred was the most brilliant and the most temperamental of the writers in the colony and my favorite eccentric. He went mad in Tangier and died in Jerusalem.

Some of the writers earned rent money by writing pornographic novels for Maurice Girodias of Olympia Press. But to remain in Paris indefinitely forced them to turn out many books under many pseudonyms. This taxed their ingenuity at inventing juicy vices. Such books were sold, Girodias confided, largely to the British armed forces.

After I hounded him relentlessly Trocchi agreed to publish my poetry collection, *An Almanac for Amorists*, under the Merlin imprint, a highbrow subsidiary of the Olympia Press of which he was editor. A heroin addict from Glasgow, Trocchi accepted the book but did nothing about printing it. Fortunately Kermit had rejoined me in Paris and he assumed responsibility for the project. Despite coming to blows more than once with an irritable printer who hated the English language Kermit designed and illustrated a handsome volume which Barney Rosset picked up for distribution by Grove Press.

That winter of 1955 we lived on the top floor of Raymond Duncan's Akademia building in the rue de Seine, where he still held court in Greek costume attended by three of his ex-wives. To enter our apartment you first stepped into the shower, then passed through the kitchen to reach the bed-sitting room. In the roofless toilet down the hall, one could sit open to the sky and watch the rats running along the gutters of the roof and feel the snow falling on one's head.

The most endearing person I met in Paris was Princess Marguerite Caetani. A civilized and discerning lady in her seventies, she published in Rome a sizable trilingual literary quarterly called *Botteghe Oscure*, named after the Roman street on which stood the Palazzo Caetani. She had accepted some poems of mine which John Davenport had sent her, and when she came to Paris to visit her friend Rene Char and meet new writers, she summoned me to her apartment near the American embassy. I immediately fell in love with her.

An American heiress happily married many years to an Italian prince, literate and discerning in her frail elegance, invariably wearing sweaters and pearls and sensible shoes, Marguerite could have been the matured heroine of a Henry James novel. With luncheons and francs she nourished many budding authors in Paris and cared for their well-being. When I came down with dysentery after a trip to Morocco she paid the doctor bills, as she had also paid for Alfred Chester's appendectomy.

Marguerite was enthusiastic about the long dramatic poem I was working on, my *True & False Unicorn*, a "portrait of the poet as a

unicorn" that had engrossed me for several years. When Kermit and I
went to Italy in the spring of 1955 seeking a quiet place to write,
Marguerite offered us rent-free haven in an unoccupied castle belong-
ing to her husband. Upon the recent death of his older brother Prince
Rodolfo Caetani had inherited the title Duke of Sermoneta as well as
the town that went with it. Sermoneta was a fortified hill-town with
a medieval castle that overlooked the campana near Anzio.

We took the train from Rome south to the tiny station at Ninfa
where the Caetanis had a country estate. Marguerite met us in a
Ford station wagon. Her chauffeur drove us up the winding road to
picturesquely walled Sermoneta. The towers of the castle and its
drawbridge over a dry ditch promised romantic atmosphere, but
once the high creaking doors had been unlocked by a dusty custodian the interior dashed our dream. The castle was furnished with
nothing but a dank smell and thick cobwebs, had neither electricity
nor running water, and was populated by innumerable bats. "I
didn't think you'd like it," said the Duchess of Sermoneta. "Let's go
down to Ninfa and have lunch with Rodolfo."

Still questing a congenial summer haven Kermit and I went on to
Naples, deciding to visit Wystan Auden on the island of Ischia. That
year Auden was translating *The Magic Flute* into English for NBC,
waiting for Chester Kallman to return from Greece, listening to
Callas sing Bellini on his gramophone, and holding court every
night at Maria's café in the town square with outrageous anecdotes
of everyone we'd ever heard of and never met. I remember his
denunciations of Brecht: "I will provide him with an excellent dinner, and then shoot him. After all, he is a Kraut." And he often
advised me: "Never forget what Alice's friend Mabel said, 'Keep
your toes well turned out, if you don't know the English word use
the French, and always remember who you are.'"

Wystan persuaded Maria to let us occupy the rooms she owned
in the town's water tower, and there we spent the summer looking
out over the harbor and hobnobbing with both the resident and the

seasonal natives. The latter included Hans Werner Henze, Anthony Hecht, Iris Tree, William Walton, and a Belgian painter of large abstractions who had an excellent recipe for stuffed octopus. That summer in Forio included more beachside idleness than we needed. Kermit took to drawing pictures of local boys in the nude and I found myself writing poems of considerable uneasiness.

> Is inert sorrow plugged in to stay?
> A plow to break the otiose, please!
> Sumptuous or not, the terraces for summer ribaldry
> revive the odor of dead desire...

My blithe facade had begun to show some cracks. Writing *True & False Unicorn* had challenged me to accept my inborn oddity: "Hallelujah for the living thing unique!" it sang. Once I had completed this probing work (after Auden suggested some prosodic emendations) and sent it to Marguerite for publication, my reason for remaining abroad came into question.

Antics such as I had cooked up in the Crystal Palace Gardens had come to seem delusionary and irrelevant. Had I strayed too far from what my angel had once asked of me in the middle of the night? Was that why I had begun to slide into undiagnosable ailments: spasms, sags, and cramps? The immediate question arose: was it time to revisit some roots?

A return to California might mean some kind of new beginning. But the prospect sent a chill through me. I remember how much of a chill because when Kermit and I took the drafty boat train for the S. S. *Liberté* in late November, Mary McCarthy sat opposite me blowing her nose all the way to Cherbourg.

8

IN THE TIME OF GURUS

WHEN KERMIT and I returned to San Francisco in December of 1955 we walked into a new literary vortex spinning around the North Beach coffee houses. Details of the Beat Scene we soon learned from Lawrence Ferlinghetti who lived near the cottage we rented on Telegraph Hill. Lawrence had published in the *San Francisco Chronicle* a kind review of my *Almanac* and he introduced us to the new arrivals on the poetic scene: Philip Whalen, Gary Snyder, Gregory Corso, and the highly vocal leader of the group, Allen Ginsberg. Ferlinghetti's newly opened City Lights Bookstore had become a meeting place for poets, browsers, and avant-garde book thieves.

When Lawrence published *Howl* he and Ginsberg's book were brought to trial for indecency, thereby gaining international notoriety. When I first met him Ginsberg carried around mimeographed copies of the poem which he read aloud loudly wherever he went. He had already acquired a reputation for taking off his clothes at proper social gatherings, the properer the sooner he disrobed. When we invited Allen to dinner he kept his clothes on but he brought along his new boyfriend, Peter Orlovsky, who put his feet up on the table right into the butter dish. "Think nothing of it," said Allen, "Peter is a saint." Peter called me Brautigan that night in 1956 and has continued to do so ever since. "No," Allen will say to him every time we encounter, "This is Broughton, not Brautigan."

Following Allen's example the Beat poets gave public performances that were more political and more salacious than those of ten years before. Some of us in the older avant-garde — Rexroth, Duncan, Everson, even Josephine Miles — were swept onto the Beat roller coaster simply by residing in the neighborhood. Of younger talents I was entranced by Michael McClure's intensity while Jack Spicer did not forgive my aversion to bridge and baseball. Joanne Kyger complained that the Beat poets who flopped at her pad were too stoned to do any fucking. Whalen was the Buddha of the lot, Corso the imp, and Snyder the Coyote. Ferlinghetti had the most authentic smile.

Though I was an admiring friend to these poets I have never been identified with any literary group for long. Besides, at this time my snarled energies needed therapeutic attention more than literary competition. I didn't want to admit I was at a neurotic impasse. Does anyone? Not wanting to inflict my irritabilities on Kermit, I encouraged him to become full-time director of the theater company that he loved. He was happy to move into his theater building and sleep in the green room. In no way did this close off our collaborating. Over the next fifteen years we worked together on theater pieces and film projects.

To soothe my quandaries and cramps I sought experts in massage, tarot, and yoga. I also visited churches. In Europe I had often found solace in religious architectures. Of these the most impressive had been the shrine of Santiago de Compostela in Spain, where in July of 1954 I discovered an affinity for my namesake saint, James the son of Zebedee, patron of Spain, alchemists, and explorers. I adopted his scallop shell and his pilgrim staff as my own emblems.

Back in San Francisco I visited every church dedicated to St. James, then proceeded to those of other saints. One afternoon I wandered into Grace Cathedral which I had not entered for twenty years. A vesper service was under way in the chapel, the tall red and blue windows over the high altar glowed in the sunset light. As I knelt at the altar rail a wall inside me suddenly gave way and deluged me with tears. What tidal wave of old sorrows was this?

Waking alone on the sunny November morning of my forty-third birthday, I felt despair trying to choke me. Longing for an expanse of open air I set out for Land's End at the shore of the Pacific. Along the trail of the headland high above the Golden Gate I met no one. I walked toward the edge of the continent, hoping to inhale fresh enthusiasm.

But I was forced back. The trail abruptly ceased where the unstable shale of the cliff had collapsed. When I retraced my steps I discovered that at one perpendicular gully much of my return trail had also collapsed. This confronted me with a gap of some eight feet between the point where I stood and where the path began again. When I had casually skipped over this on the way westward I had loosened much of the gravel. The gap now required a gazelle leap. My legs, remembering only their fleet dancing days, took a long unthinking jump.

But where I landed the trail disintegrated under my feet. When I reached out to grab support the cliff-side came away in my hands and I slipped down the steep incline at the mercy of falling pebbles. I tried to press my body against the crumbling cliff but I kept sliding closer toward the precipice. My feet already hung out in midair. The drop that awaited me would hurl me a thousand feet down upon the jagged rocks that lined the shore of the Golden Gate.

Was gravity determined to pull me toward a shattering dismemberment? No no! Didn't I have half my life yet to live? Even at the risk of death shouldn't I attempt an impossible last leap?

Very slowly I pulled up each leg and braced my feet against the slope as if they actually had sure footing. Calling on all the gods I could think of I flung myself across the gully. Miraculously my arms landed where I could scramble up slippery shale and crawl onto solid ground. I lay panting in disbelief. Only the grace of some divine arms could have lifted me to safety. Did these belong to Hermy, the angelic guardian of my fate?

Such a narrow escape forced me to recognize the precariousness of my inner balance. No drugstore potions nor Episcopal prayers would make enough difference. I would have to locate a doctor for my soul. Fortunately I found my way to the skillful sympathies of Joseph Henderson, dean of Jungian analysts in San Francisco, a ceremonious mandarin both worldly and down-to-earth. He had been born in Elko, Nevada, and trained in Zurich. His younger brother Jack had been my classmate at Tamalpais School and a particular pal when we had adjoining rooms in the dormitory and could climb into one another's windows after Lights Out.

During five years' time Dr. Henderson led me around the circles of my own hell and brought me to a purgatory where I could come to terms with the mother who occupied my psyche like a rhinoceros trampling on my impulses and ambitions. To give full attention to expiating forty years of secret intimidation, I quit the city and took refuge in a cabin on the dunes of Stinson Beach that faced the Great Unconscious of the Pacific. My special neighbor there was Hermy, who told me I was old enough now to call him by his real name which was Hermes, Azothius of Zane. He came round often with his healing sparkler and some cautionary words.

"Take this excavation work seriously but see if you can whistle in your labyrinth. Don't forget Big Joy. We want you to be a Paul Revere poet waking up the world. It's not just your own midnight ride, you have to ride faster than the runaway nightmare of the times. Or laughter will never triumph."

While dwelling with perplexities by the sea I encountered another doctor of the soul, one who relieved my torments philosophically. Did Alan Watts and I share an immediate chuckle? Every time we met during our eighteen years of friendship we both broke into laughter. On the flyleaf of my copy of his autobiography Alan calligraphed this Zen poem in Japanese characters:

Meeting they laugh and laugh;
In the forest, fallen leaves are many.

Our conviviality began on a poetic occasion: tea at the home of poet Jean Burden where Alan, after some philosophical sallies, recited a Betjeman poem, a medieval hymn, and two anticlerical limericks. I countered with a few lyrics of my own. Henceforth before anything else, we were fellow poets. Despite being at that time dean of the American Academy of Asian Studies, Alan admitted he cherished metaphysical nonsense as a key to the Infinite. "Trailing clouds of glory do we come" was less to his taste than "'Twas brillig, and the slithy toves." From Tokyo once he sent me the following postcard:

Hum, hum the Humbledrum!
Rumbling bumbling dumbledrum,
Mumbling dumbly, rumbling humbly,
Humming mumbly, bumbling glumly,
Fumbling thumbly, tumbling clumsy,
Double-dumbled Humbledrum.

Similarly he could parody his own style of philosophic disquisition:

On the whole I prefer dongulation. It is prepid, snord, and tart, and the vallification of an estimate is grolic. Churdles and mards will always require fronicks, and lapsy daddles are usually bequeathed to the snorder kind of lumpens. Bolliworts are frankly bespoken, and every mutter-hound is a preposterous garble of tonsils.

Alan's playfulness relieved the solemnity of Jungian symbolizing. He took me through non-symbolic realms of philosophy into the superior wackiness of Zen and the sunlit moments of Taoism. I hung out with him to keep my soul in balance, sat in on his lectures, made up verses to amuse him. He adopted me as the jester poet of his private court. One year he telephoned the governor to nominate me for poet laureate of the state of California.

On January 6, 1965 Alan celebrated his fiftieth birthday with an elaborate feast aboard the S.S. *Vallejo*, the beached ferry boat in Sausalito where he was living at that time and where he presented his seminars. For that festive occasion I composed and recited a tribute, "Forget-me-nots for Alan Watts:"

Does anyone know the true wherefores and whats
of this singular person called Alan Watts?

Does he get his ideas for his seminar talks
by going on long cross-country walks, or trots,
Mr. Alan Watts?

When he writes out a chapter to confound the wise
does he cross all his T's and finish his I's with dots,
does Alan Watts?

Does he do his thinking in pontifical hats?
Does he sleep on a bed or on Japanese mats, or on cots,
this Alan Watts?

Can he write his calligraphy concisely clear
without any smudge, any speck or smear, or blots,
can Alan Watts?

Does he get his kicks by the clear blue waves
or by prowling about in dark green caves, or in grots,
the Alan of Watts?

When he grows inspired with brilliant notions
does he dance about in primitive motions, or gavottes,
Dr. Alan Watts?

Does he practice sex magic in sacred rivers?
Do beautiful women give him the shivers, or the hots?
                                        O Alan Watts!

Is it true that at birth he gave a great shout
and said, I've already figured life out in my thoughts,
                                        said Baby Watts?

Did he also remark to his parents from the crib,
Your concept of truth is a childish fib, you clots,
                                        said Little Watts?

And when he had made all his family skittish
did he then upset the rest of the British, including the Scots,
                                        did Alan Watts?

Was it in America, and do you know when
that he put down Jesus and took up Zen, and other whatnots,
                                        the Reverend Watts?

Is he now quite content with his own dominion?
Does he care not a fig for public opinion, or lots,
                                        does Alan Watts?

Is it true that he thrives on exotic drugs
which he keeps in barrels, trunks and jugs, and in pots,
                                        this Alan Watts?

Though it's said that he breakfasts on LSD,
does he swallow the stuff in his morning tea, or in shots?
                                        Why, Alan Watts!

When he gives a lecture for all to hear
does he leave his audience perfectly clear, or in knots,
                                        Professor Watts?

Alan responded to this parody in his own merry way. On my next birthday he presented me with a verse tribute he called "Birdle Burble:"

I went out of my mind and then came to my senses
By meeting a magpie who mixed up his tenses,
Who muddles distinctions of nouns and of verbs,
And insisted that logic is bad for the birds.
    With a poo-wee cluck and a chit, chit-chit,
    The grammar and meaning don't matter a bit.

The stars in their courses have no destination;
The train of events will arrive at no station;
The inmost and ultimate Self of us all
Is dancing on nothing and having a ball.
    So with chat for chit and with tat for tit,
    This will be that, and that will be It!

The last line of his poem refers to a poem of mine inspired by the publication of his book *This Is It*. This verse version of the "Suchness of Is" Alan liked so much that he quoted it at the end of his book called *The Book: On the Taboo Against Knowing Who You Are:*

This is It
and I am It
and You are It
and so is That
and He is It
and She is It
and It is It
and That is That

O It is This
and It is Thus
and It is Them
and It is Us
and It is Now
and here It is
and here We are
so This is It

That I had experienced this much awareness of enlightenment testifies to the insights that Alan had bestowed on me. He confirmed Hermy's tip that life is a sacred comedy and that "cosmic" and "comic" are interchangeable words. Alan loved to quote G. K. Chesterton's remark: "The reason angels can fly is that they take themselves lightly." He said he wanted everyday life to be permeated by "the same jazz that constitutes the cosmos." For his morning meditation Alan went out on his porch and holding his ribs with both hands laughed with the universe for ten minutes. He said that at daybreak he felt everything was radiantly in place. Sometimes by nightfall everything had fallen back into disarray. But he considered the rigidity of zazen too military a discipline for the nonstop dance of all things.

When Alan abandoned his Anglican ministry in Chicago and came to San Francisco to head the Asian Academy he still carried an aura of British stiffness. California of the sixties transformed him. There he could acknowledge that he was by nature an itinerant philosopher who loathed dogma, domesticity and propriety. When I met him he was preparing to resign from the Academy and wondering how to resign from his wife and five children. He preferred his new traveling companion Mary Jane Yates, a brassy, Wyoming-born public relations expert more devoted to career promotion than to babies.

Spiritually Alan felt closer to another woman. A serious British-born poet, a conscientious lesbian and something of a witch, Elsa

Gidlow had become a surrogate sister to him. She lived on a remote slope of Mt. Tamalpais with several cats, two goats, and a vegetable garden. This knoll with its abandoned orchard she named Druid Heights. It could be reached only by a winding one-lane dirt road above Muir Woods. Alan often escaped to Druid Heights from his tangled domesticity in Mill Valley. I went there to counteract the isolation of my retreat at Stinson Beach.

Perhaps because he had been an only child, Alan adopted Elsa and me as his poet siblings. In the years following his separation from his wife Dorothy we stood devotedly on either side of him. This is not to say that Elsa and I ever became chums. Her initial reaction to anything I said tended toward frown. When I playfully versified the sense of Zen Alan had taught me, as in "Those Old Zen Blues, or After the Seminar" Elsa accused me of making fun of him. Alan retaliated that I was the one person who really caught on to his crazy wisdom. Elsa was not convinced. She scoffed when I read aloud my metaphysical drinking song titled, "Here's to It," which begins:

Here's to that thing
we won't admit.
Here's to the omnipresent
It.
Here's to the It
in which we sit
and stand and walk
and laugh and spit.
It's in every act
that we commit.
It's our inescapable
requisite.

Elsa's response was, "Do you always use a rhyming dictionary?" I admit that I replied, "How else would I have learned to rhyme cunt and waterfront?"

Since Alan insisted on my being present when he visited her house Elsa pretended to accept me. On one occasion, however, we did share a peculiar intimacy. At her annual Christmas night gathering I was stretched dozingly on her couch after a great deal of mulled wine. The only light in the room came from the flickering Yule log. A few snores reverberated in the corners. Suddenly I felt Elsa snuggling against me, rubbing my genitals. When she slipped my cock into her vagina I was astonished by the abyss it dropped into. After this holiday exchange Elsa expressed greater cordiality toward both me and my poetry.

Despite her customary sobriety Druid Heights in those years became a center of revelry. This was fomented by Elsa's neighbor Roger Somers, the other major inhabitant of the hilltop. If Elsa was the vestal priestess and I the joking minstrel, Roger was the master of the revels, and his revels tended toward the orgiastic. This husky blond laughing cabinetmaker who abhorred straight lines had converted the interior of a nondescript farmhouse into a sinuous Oriental temple. He also played a fiendish saxophone, a heavenly oboe, and bloodcurdling drums. Alan treasured Roger's merriment and adopted him as his Dionysian major-domo. Though he had maintained a continuing traffic in wives and lovers, Roger was temperamentally as unattached as Elsa and I. Alan considered our quaternity his special enlightened family.

In the imaginative playground of Druid Heights Alan's amanuensis Mary Jane (whom he called Jano) seemed often out of place. But she devoted herself to promoting Alan and his image. In their marriage she functioned as his noncritical drinking companion and his partner in sexual experiment. In this she differed markedly from his previous wives. As time went on, however, she tended to overimbibe and spend more time knocked out than awake. Alan himself slept very little. He began writing every morning at five.

In addition to Roger's nocturnal frolics we also partook of unusual meals. Alan liked to putter in Elsa's kitchen and cook unnecessary delicacies like *paté en croute*, plum pudding, and green marijuana layer cake. One summer day in 1959 on the sun deck of Elsa's house Alan served an unforgettable luncheon to his intimates: Roger and his then wife Barbara, Elsa and myself, Alan's daughter Anne and her harpist husband Joel Andrews. The menu: LSD pills direct from Dr. Albert Hoffman's laboratory in Switzerland. This was a first experience for all of us except Alan who had been inducted at Harvard by Professor Timothy Leary. Since no public information about the drug existed at that time we neophytes did not know what to expect. Would it be enlightenment by sunset or death by morning? The actuality was both of these and more. I don't remember what the others did but I remember crawling through Elsa's zucchini patch, finding enormous strawberries like edible jewels and suddenly coming upon Roger's bare feet. These were so splendidly formed and powerful I believed they must be the feet of the god Shiva. To offset being trampled by them I kissed them in ecstatic awe. That was only the beginning of an extraordinary day of transformations and terrors that concluded with Alan serving a communion of ordinary bread and wine that seemed under the circumstances the most delectable edibles I had ever tasted.

In that year other magical trips took place on the mountain. Alan's book *The Joyous Cosmology*, wherein Roger is called Robert, describes some of the most memorable of those visionary days and nights when I encountered grinning spiders on burning clouds and participated in Roger's ever inventive games.

My awe before Roger's feet extended to his whole being. He was as much Pan as Shiva, a slyly merry begetter and destroyer. He also possessed the gift of compassion. He responded to my affection for him by bringing Barbara down to my beach cottage one evening and urging the three of us into bed together. Thus I was able to explore the rest of Shiva's body as well as that of his consort and so connect with their essences. I would have liked to connect as familiarly with Alan as I had with Elsa and Roger. But Alan kept his arm at arm's length. Until the night of a certain dinner party.

Barbara often prepared surprising feasts in Roger's phallic-shaped kitchen. Though she appeared to be a contented woodland nymph, one day she said goodbye to Roger and soon after turned up in New York on the staff of *Gourmet* magazine. Following one of her last banquets on the mountain the surfeited guests sprawled lazily on the tatami while Alan took potshots at Jung's theory of the Collective Unconscious. As he stretched out, he dropped his drunken head into my lap and went on talking with his eyes shut. I began to caress his brow with one hand and rub his neck with the other. He reached for my hand saying, "Why don't we go to Zurich together and really show them what the Unconscious is all about?" I leaned over and kissed him on his brow. He squeezed my hand and passed out. I looked across the room and caught Roger's grinning wink.

Alan liked to describe himself as a connoisseur of Port and Bordeaux. Actually he was more partial to vodka. And vodka came to be his daily necessity. He said, "When I drink I don't feel so alone." Paying substantial alimonies to support ex-wives and children while maintaining his own lifestyle with Jano required him to make frequent lecture tours and produce as many books as he could turn out. Vodka helped him maintain the cheerful front of an enlightened sage.

His addiction to vodka equaled that of George Gamow. Vulnerable Barbara Perkins, my once roommate in Greenwich Village, had ended up in Boulder the wife of the forceful physicist who invented the "Big Bang." When I was their houseguest George Gamow would not allow me morning coffee until I had downed at least three shots of straight vodka. While I steeled myself to swallow the dose, George declaimed Pushkin in Russian. However giddy he might feel, he could proceed to the University of Colorado and deliver a sober lecture on the expanding universe. Similarly Alan Watts could come unsteadily onto a stage and perform a lucid exposition of Hindu cosmology. But the constitution of even the sturdiest

Muscovite or Anglican has its breaking point. Both George Gamow and Alan Watts owe their early deaths to vodka.

I survived my own vodka period when I was living once again in San Francisco. During my last year of depth analysis so many demons had escaped from my Shadow to terrorize my nights that I once called the police to rout intruders prowling over my head in an attic that did not exist. After such traumas I would sit in my kitchen window overlooking Union Street and drink vodka until dawn. Alcoholism, however, was not to be my fate. Another and younger kind of soul doctor would soon join me in that apartment and revitalize my ability to love.

For his part Alan suffered great difficulty expressing love or surrendering to it. Not only had he inherited frigidities from his mother, but his erotic pleasure had been long connected with pain — a legacy from canings received in British schools. Whenever he came down the mountainside from Druid Heights to visit my cottage on the dunes I would get him to splash in the surf, swing kelp whips, chase sandpipers, gather treasures from the deep. I enjoyed him most when his intellect dozed and we renewed our poetic games.

One afternoon at Stinson Beach in the absence of his usual entourage Alan and I shared a more intimate exchange. After frolicking along the sands the two of us were enjoying drinks on the deck of my cottage. Alan was talking about the Tao and how to "go with" the flow of everything. He said, "It's hard for people to get hold of this idea because it means letting go."

That prompted me to speak of something long on my mind, "Alan, how does one take hold of a concept? I don't know anything unless I can feel it. How can I hold the Tao in my hands? How can I caress the Holy Spirit? I would like to touch ideas, smell them, see how they taste. I would also like to embrace those whose minds have touched me."

Alan gave a muffled laugh and knit his brow. But having gone this far I had to continue: "I would like to hold your ideas in my arms. I would like to feel the breath of your wisdom in my ear. Can we ever close the intellect door and open the love window?" There was a long pause. Finally I said, "Okay. I will settle for a good hug."

Alan gave my arm a perfunctory squeeze. "This is something new to me. If ever I could enjoy sex with another man, it would surely be with someone like you."

"I'm not talking about sex, Alan. I'm talking about how to experience the heart of your mind. I dreamt that you came to my bed and lay alongside me all night. This deeply comforted me, as if I were lying close to the truth of things."

Alan said, "That's a beautiful idea. I'm touched."

"Where? Where does it touch you?" I asked. "A tingle in your soul? An itch in your balls?"

"The Chinese believe the soul is in the big toe."

"Why not in your genitals? Isn't that where the divine mystery operates?"

Tittering thoughtfully Alan went to get another vodka. When he returned, I asked him, "If you don't agree about the soul, where in the body is the Unconscious?"

"Jung never answered that one," replied Alan. "But since the Unconscious is a glutton for symbolic smorgasbords it must reside in the guts."

I confided to him how childhood disturbances had racked my guts, how on any motor trip in my stepfather's car I would hear my mother's irritation: "Stop the car! Jimmy's throwing up again." And now this present conversation was giving me intestinal cramps. When emotionally aroused I am prone to sudden attacks of diarrhea. I asked Alan to put his hand on my stomach to quiet the pain. He backed away.

Not only did intimacy with another man confound Alan Watts, eventually women too confounded him. In the year before he died we had another private conversation, this time at Druid Heights when we were soaking in Roger's redwood hot tub. Never before had I heard him express personal disillusionments. When it came to women he had loved he felt most devoted to his two daughters, Joan and Anne. He had come to feel that all three of his marriages had been more burden than elation. He had even wearied of the transient pleasure of taking to bed female devotees on his lecture tours.

As he looked toward the mountain beyond the eucalyptus grove he deplored, in almost a whisper, the necessity of having to have any mate at all. He confessed that at this point in his life he would prefer to be a self-sufficient hermaphrodite able to fuck himself. He went on to speculate whether every man might be happier if such self-love were possible. God, he thought, had made a great error with human anatomy by making self-fellatio so physically difficult. A pity, he added, that dogs don't seem to appreciate how fortunate they are in their flexibility. After all, didn't masturbation provide the most satisfactory sex? And especially as one grew older.

I have heard two other men in their fifties say much the same thing, men who had indulged in ample womanizing and a full share of parenting but found later contentment in a return to playing with their fantasies. Is this a normal way to enter second childhood?

As the burdens of his public life increased Alan began to spend more time at Druid Heights. Roger had built him a library there, and alongside it a cottage in the shape of an apple. Of this refuge he wrote in his last book, *Cloud-Hidden, Whereabouts Unknown.*

It was in the apple house that he asked me to collaborate with him on a special project. He thought the subject so explosive that it demanded a dramatic form. He was uncertain whether it should be a play or a novel, neither of which he had ever written. "It will be called *The Guru*," he confided gleefully. "I want to expose the hypocritical shenanigans in the whole guru business. I've known them all. What a ball we'll have writing this! We can let every fat religious cat out of the bag. What a scandal we'll create!"

Alan had come to believe that he himself, like everyone else in public life, could be characterized as "a successful fake." It was everybody's story, he said ruefully: "a confused little embryo learns to bluff his way into being taken for a person of competence."

I knew little about the guru business, I had encountered only a few. A grandiose one was Bhagwan Shree Rajneesh. In 1984 Joel Singer and I were the invited guests of Rajneesh at his humongous Utopia in the desert of eastern Oregon. We were housed in an A-frame cottage in what was called, invitingly enough, Alan Watts Grove at Basho Pond. Before he left Poona Rajneesh had written to me praising my *High Kukus*. Subsequently he had taken the title for one of his many books from a sentence in my *Seeing the Light*: "Zen: Zip, Zap, and Zing." At Rajneeshpurim we feasted at Zorba the Buddha Buffet, swam in Lake Krishnamurti, admired the farm and the airport, and visited the large bookshop containing only books by Rajneesh.

Asthmatic velvet-robed Bhagwan provided a markedly different figure from Chogyam Trungpa Rimpoche, snappily dapper in Western business suits with cufflinks, silk neckties, and carefully lacquered hair. Promptly at the announced hour of 2 p.m. Rajneesh drove by in one of his twenty-two Rolls Royces, whereas Trungpa was never less than an hour late for a promised appearance and then while speaking enigmatically of the Unknowable he repeatedly refreshed himself from a large decanter of gin. Alan admitted to me that he seldom understood anything Trungpa said but it always sounded impressive. Trungpa garnered public notoriety at his Naropa Institute in Boulder when he used his religious authority to intimidate and seduce his students.

Another incarnate lama, Rimpoche Tartang Tulku, had an endearing ambition to construct the largest prayer wheel in the world. At his Nyngma ashram in Berkeley he installed a huge one powered by electricity that rumbled day and night. He then constructed one the size of a silo at his meditation retreat in the wild hills of Sonoma County, believing that the evils of the USA required the sending aloft of a vast quantity of prayers.

Since Alan had participated often in what he called "gaggles of gurus" I looked forward to hearing his scandalous stories. But we never wrote a word of this exposé. The day I came to begin the collaboration at Druid Heights I found Alan in the woods nearby wearing a Japanese fireman's jacket and brandishing a tall samurai bow. He was shooting deadly arrows into the air straight over his head. He laughed wildly as he waited to see how close to him each arrow would fall. As for our project he proposed beginning it as soon as he returned from a European lecture tour. Before he sent me home that day he bestowed on me his pearl-handled walking stick and his silver Episcopate cross. That was the last time I saw Alan Watts alive.

Alan had promised to be present at the San Francisco Museum of Art for the ceremony celebrating my sixtieth birthday in November 1973. He insisted that he wanted to speak from the stage because he had something "very important to say publicly" about me. But he had returned from Europe in a state of exhaustion from liver collapse. Just before I went up on the stage at the Museum I was handed a message. I choked up when I announced that Alan Watts had died that morning.

A week later a first interment of ashes took place in front of his library at Druid Heights. I remember the invocation by Ram Dass and the flute playing of Al Chung-liang Huang. Then in Buddhist tradition on the one-thousandth day after his death his remaining ashes were interred beneath a stone stupa on a hillside above the Zen Center's Green Gulch Farm in Marin County. On that sunny afternoon a procession of local pundits, priests, and personages climbed the hill. Crippled Lama Govinda, wearing his Tibetan red and gold robes, was carried on a litter like the image of a saint. Widow Jano, several of Alan's children, Gary Snyder, and I were those asked to lift with chopsticks one or two small bones from the funerary urn and deposit them into the earth. Richard Baker-Roshi officiated at the ceremony and gave Alan a Buddhist name, Yu Zen Myo Ko, which he said meant "Profound mountain, Subtle light."

Gary read a poem evoking Alan, and then I read the elegy I had written the day after Alan's death:

He was a gleeful metaphysician.
He loved nature, man, and woman, and their joyous cosmology.
He was a scholar and a gentleman who loved to take down his
   hair and kick up his heels.
He traveled beyond theology.
He had shaken the two hands of God.
He understood the meaning of happiness and the wisdom of
   insecurity.
He was a sensual bishop and an impish Bodhisattva.
He loved ritual and ribaldry and the ridiculous.
He was a star drummer for the dance of life.
He loved the music of Yes and No singing together.
He knew that the only way to hold on is to let go.
He knew the way of Zen, the way of Tao,
   the way it is, the way it might be
   and he knew it in his own way
   which is the only way to make it known.
There are those who can dance on a pin and those who can
   pinpoint the dance.
Alan Watts could do both.

9

A WEDDING AND A WEDDING

WHEN ALAN Watts died my wife said, "Now that we have lost our family priest, who will I get to officiate at your funeral?" Such flippancy was characteristic of Suzanna. Yet it was true that Alan had officiated at our wedding, at the christening of our two children, at holidays and birthdays. As for the wedding, since I had waited till age forty-nine to explore marriage, I wanted the experience to be as substantial as a three-act play. Not surprisingly, it grew into a three-day event. This took place in December of 1962.

On the first day we said our civil vows at high noon to a judge in the City Hall of San Francisco, where I still bled from the shaving cut I had given myself that morning. Later that day we drove north to my friend Bill Brewer's romantic inn at Cuffey's Cove on the Mendocino Coast. There the year before his hospitality had sustained me through a crucial transformation of my soul which I described in *The Androgyne Journal*. Now he turned over his entire cliff-side haven to our celebration. Down at the cove on our second ritual day Suzanna and I enacted a joint transformation ceremony. We tossed into the sea photos, love letters, and miscellaneous souvenirs of our past peccadilloes and discarded follies, asking the deep waters to accept these sacrifices and bestow upon us in return a clear new wave of adventure.

By the third day a select group of guests had arrived for the climactic occasion: the Latin nuptial mass (with poetic additions of my own) performed by Alan, attended by Jano and Barbara Somers as his acolytes. Roger Somers had come along to play his oboe and Joel Andrews with his harp spun variations on "Come Ye Sons of Art." Kermit served as my best man, while both our Jungian analysts also stood with us: Elizabeth Osterman for Suzanna and Joseph Henderson for me. I needed as much friendly support as I could muster.

One other person present, not a familiar of the Watts or the Jungian circles, had been crucial in promoting this marriage. Furthermore he had offered to record the activities of these three days with his 16 millemeter camera. He was the prominent young filmmaker Stan Brakhage.

By this year of 1962 Brakhage was not only an influential avant-garde artist, he had also become a major influence on my life. I had first met him in New York in 1956 after my return from the years in Europe. At an Eighth Street bar Willard Maas introduced him with characteristic exaggeration, as "the biggest genius in the country with the smallest equipment."

I was excited by the creative fire that roared in him. A heavyset *enfant terrible*, Brakhage was taller than I but twenty years younger, with tortured brows, delicate nostrils, and graceful hands. Delighted to meet me, he said, "This is a great moment in my life," and explained how he had come to San Francisco from Denver in 1951 with the prime intention of meeting me, only to discover that I had gone to England. For him I was a "master" in the field that he would make the focus of his life. Duncan had let him sleep in the

Centaur Press basement where he found a discarded print of *Mother's Day* which he projected frequently on the white water heater. For my poetry he expressed as much admiration as for my cinema, claiming to be a frustrated poet himself.

Of his life he spoke with histrionic emphasis: how he had been born in Kansas, an orphan who never knew his real parents, had been adopted by an incompatible couple who moved to Denver and parked him in movie houses for his babysitting. He nurtured a fantasy that his natural father might have been Thomas Wolfe. Certainly he possessed Wolfeian fevers of ambition and sentiment. His personal charm was so expansive that it quite captured my heart. But he was about to return to Colorado to marry his sweetheart. I was returning to California to do I knew not what.

In the years that followed I saw Brakhage whenever he came to the Bay Area and more than once he brought me to Boulder to give readings and show my films at the University of Colorado. There he persuaded his wife Jane to perform my "Ballad of Mad Jenny," and he constantly urged me to resume film work. By the time he came to stay with me in San Francisco in the early spring of 1961 he had fathered three daughters and twenty films.

I had arranged some local lectures for Brakhage and invited him to stay with me in my Union Street flat. I had relinquished my isolation at the beach in order to return to the stimulus of artists and the arts. In this regard Brakhage proved a significant inspiration. During his two-week stay he became spry, jocular, and each day more compassionate. I thought him the most ardent man ever to come out of Kansas. And he talked and talked and we both talked at the same time, discussing the impossible possibilities of creative life. Often we sat far into the night around the oak table in my kitchen window, snacks of meat and cheese between us, glasses of wine and brandy, trays of cigarette butts.

One evening he surprised me by saying, "Oh, what I see! Such great things are locked up in you, James, crying out to be unbolted.

Such wonderful things! But you have an iron band around your head. Right across here." He ran his hands across my forehead. "It must hurt. It keeps you from being your true dancing self. How can we get rid of it? I wish I had the power. It would be the greatest gift I could give you. I'll try. Maybe I can loosen it a little." And he held my head in both his hands as he searched my eyes with such intensity that I expected my head would burst into a full-blown lotus.

I was sorry that it didn't. I was ready for a new cycle of life, ready to find a new collaborating comrade. And here was a younger man rewaking my enthusiasm for art and for life. Furthermore, unlike Alan Watts or Dr. Henderson, Brakhage put loving hands upon me. He not only stroked my brow to rid it of its fears, he embraced me sympathetically and came into my bed and let me love him. One day he went out and bought me a set of film rewinds and said, "There! Doesn't that inspire you?"

My heart had leapt over the moon and everything else in the sky. But how could I expect prolonged intimacy or creative collaboration with such a self-sufficient genius and dedicated family man?

To cushion my ardor and divert Stan I invited a lively neighbor to join our evenings. For some time Suzanna Hart had been my most entertaining companion. She had moved to a Union Street apartment when her husband deserted her for a French banker. He had also deserted the debts of his theater in Berkeley where, as well as being his wife, Suzanna had been his leading lady and leading designer. Now she worked for the San Francisco Opera, mixing and applying makeups for stars and supers and superstars.

Suzanna was as theatrical offstage as on. When Kermit first introduced me to her years before at the opening night of my revue, *The Rites of Women*, she wore a blue wig, blue makeup, blue stockings, blue beads, and blue nail polish. She said, "One must always improve on nature." She was petite, perky, as colorful and challenging as a fluffy thistle. Since exaggeration was her style, she spoke as if she were auditioning for the role of Gwendolyn in *The*

Importance of Being Earnest. She addressed me: "Oh you fascinating man!" and sent me fan letters with quotes from *The White Goddess* and e.e cummings.

But now, divorced and nearing forty, she had put aside wigs and taken up Jung. She recognized her need for a new direction, but didn't know what it was. We shared these challenges in late night chats. Her tongue remained incorrigibly mischievous and this flirtatious waggery enchanted Brakhage. He was pleased to learn that she had been born in Wichita. He insisted that as a fellow Kansan she must have felt blessed like him by such proximity to the land of Oz, ignoring her insistence that she hated the Oz books.

When Brakhage departed for Colorado to go back to his wife and daughters, he left me feeling exhausted and confused. At the moment of goodbye when I reached to hug him, he said, "You and Suzie have such fun. Why do you have separate flats in the same block? Couldn't you move in together?"

I persuaded Suzanna to go to the mountains the following weekend. In my VW Beetle we got as far as Sonora Pass where we shared a narrow bed in a log cabin motel. She was surprised by the force of my desire: "I thought you and Stan were having a big thing, the way you two were carrying on." Though I explained that my passion had cooled I clung to the illusion that I could maintain some kind of liaison with Brakhage. To this end I kept up a persistent correspondence.

During the summer of 1962 he uprooted his family, piled Jane, three little girls and seven cats, camera equipment and household goods into an aged sedan with a U-Haul trailer and drove them over the Rockies and the Sierras. Jane wept at leaving her goats, but Brakhage argued that the Bay Area would be more productive for them both.

The Brakhage stay in San Francisco proved disastrous. They could afford only a waterless flat in the depths of the Mission since Brakhage sought patronage rather than employment. His cheerier moments happened in Suzanna's company. He prized the attention she gave Jane and the little girls, whom she showered with trinkets and treats. I began to see Suzanna through his appreciative eyes. I remember the crucial occasion of that crucial autumn when the light changed all around her. It was at the San Francisco Zoo.

Picnics were Suzanna's liveliest area of hostessing. She much preferred snacking to dining. One October day she proposed that we picnic with the Brakhage family at the San Francisco Zoo. On a lawn overlooking the polar bear pits she spread pretty cloths and pillows and hampers and thermoses as well as party favors and little toys. Like a merry-minded Lady Bountiful she enchanted the children and provoked guffaws from Brakhage and awe from Jane. Beholding the glow in Suzanna as she put salami and cheese together I heard myself asking myself: if you married her, James, would your life become a full-time picnic? This question so needled my symptomatic stomach that I tossed most of my sandwich to the bears. That night I insisted she stay with me in my flat.

All marriages require arrangements of some kind. And even a sissy can walk to an altar. The Jungians had convinced me where my mother had failed. Their argument used fancier terms: one could not achieve psychic wholeness until one had outgrown being a *puer* and undergone the initiation of an alchemical *coniunctio*. In other words, only by belittling the energies of Pan and Peter Pan and agreeing to cohabit and copulate could one attain the desirable conformity my mother had cherished. In my case, aside from being a surrender to the maw of the Great Mother, could wedlock justify the cost of my analysis, surprise my friends, and gratify Brakhage? He had said that he would like to see me as happy with Suzanna as he was with Jane. Though weary of the anxieties of singleness I wondered whether I was sufficiently individuated to take on the anxieties of coupling.

Suzanna did not appear a serious threat. Her realities were as make-believe as my own and we were both used to playing parts. She should have been the sister to share my boyhood theatricals

instead of Cross-eyed Jane or Gloria Zander. Due to her own ana-
lytic sessions she had abandoned her flapper image, put her hair up,
adopted peasant dresses, and gone to James Hillman seminars. She
was trying out for "fulfillment as a woman" and I was studying for
the role of "manhood." Why couldn't we be co-stars in this drama?

So we began amusing ourselves with wedding plans, elaborating
them with symbolic flourishes. For two theater-trained graduates of
Jungian mythologies the only way either of us could accept the marriage was to think of it as a major performance piece embellished
with enough flair to impress ourselves that it was for real. In order
to manage a honeymoon before Christmas we chose as a marriage
date the Feast of the Immaculate Conception, a "holy day of obliga-
tion," to be followed by the bridal suite at La Fonda in Santa Fe,
plus an overnight at the Grand Canyon Lodge.

The civil ceremony had not unnerved me unduly. For one thing, it
was short. Before the long religious ceremony in Mendocino, however, I realized I was confronting the most intimidating experience
since my entry into military school forty years before. Joel Andrews
was already playing the processional when anxiety threw my guts
into such turmoil that I told Dr. Henderson I couldn't go through
with it. He slipped me a Seconal on the way to the altar and I managed to stand upright throughout the religious service. Then Bill
Brewer served an elaborate feast to all the guests. Early in the
course of the meal I blanked out, thanks to having diluted the
Seconal with great gulps of champagne. I revived only as the assembled company escorted the newlyweds to the wedding chamber and
scattered rose petals over them. Then I passed out again. In the
morning Suzanna said, "Well, you certainly made a spectacle of
yourself last night, throwing your arms around Brakhage, kissing
Roger and Joel while they were trying to play Mozart, and weeping
all over everyone else." I denied everything.

Years later using the rewinds he had given me I edited the scenes
of our three ceremonies that Brakhage had filmed. Rather proudly I

sent the result to him. To my dismay, he replied that he considered the film, like the wedding itself, a sad black comedy. Some elements of farce had certainly entered into our drama. Nevertheless we kept the show running.

When we began to have misgivings about our performances as Hubby and Wifey we discovered new roles to play: Papa and Mama. A daughter we named Serena was born on the day of JFK's assassination. Two years later she was joined by a brother we named Orion. And the four of us lived under the redwoods of Mill Valley. The babies were adorable and amusing, like all babies. They were also creative geniuses until they went to school. I learned how to change a diaper, push a pram, and crawl on the floor taking Polaroids. I also learned what my mother found out: children seldom behave the way you want them to. But I knew better than to interfere with their uniqueness.

Parenthood turned me into a more serious wage earner. In the Creative Arts Department at San Francisco State University I taught cinema studies and ritual magic. Also I published my poetry collection, *A Long Undressing*, performed its songs to Joel Andrews' harp, and wrote plays for Kermit to produce. He had married his leading actress. Suzanna pursued her design work and painting and drew amusing pictures for an American version of *The Right Playmate*. Our collaborations otherwise focused largely on kiddie entertainments.

Teaching film history refocused my enthusiasm for movie making. Using optical effects I dressed up Brakhage's wedding footage with alchemical symbols to make it look more convincing and called the result *Nuptiae*. To make it sound more transcendent I asked Lou Harrison to compose one of his melodious scores. I had loved Lou and his music ever since hearing a concert he gave with John Cage back in 1941 when they were fresh from the Cornish School in Seattle. At Cornish Lou had complained of John's greediness in stealing Merce Cunningham away from him when John already had a wife.

My impatience to create film poetry again received a surprise cat-
alyst from Belgium. Jacques Ledoux of the Royl Belgian
Cinemathèque had come to San Francisco seeking new works for
his forthcoming World Film Exposition IV in Knokke-le-zoute during January of 1968. He pled with me to make a new film for him. I
loved sensuous and urbane Ledoux, who had been a generous friend
to me in Brussels. Not only had he honored *Mother's Day* at his
Exposition of 1948, he had been the first on the continent to show
Loony Tom when in 1951 he inserted it impulsively between
Nanook of the North and *Tabu* on a Flaherty program. He had also
invited me to be on his international jury in 1963 where I sat
between Jørgen Roos and Norman MacLaren for a memorable
week which included a showing of *The Pleasure Garden*. After his
visit in the spring of 1967 he sent me a large box of Gevart film
stock which sat on my desk like a gauntlet he had flung. Taking
baby pictures was the busiest filming I had done since 1953.

Unbeknownst to me Hermy was playing his synchronicity games.
A perky young redhead bounced into my office one afternoon,
greeted me with praise and offered his services as cameraman whenever I should need one. Fire danced in his Leo eyes and eagerness
galvanized his body. He had escaped from family proprieties in St.
Louis and from film studies at Stanford in order to embrace hippie
life in San Francisco.

As he had bounced in, so he bounced out. Taking his leave he
leapt to the window and jumped. By the time I reached it, anticipat-
ing the sight of his bloody remains two floors below, he stood in the
street waving to me and grinning. I knew then and there that I had
found a collaborator who could take me flying. Thus Bill Desloge
became my acrobatic agitator that summer of 1967. Ever fearless of
limb he was indifferent to gravity: I photographed him flying through
the air the same day he filmed me as a naked sage with a snake.

That year of 1967 had begun with the great psychedelic Be-In in
Golden Gate Park launched by old friends Ginsberg, Snyder, and

McClure, then progressed to the Summer of Love in Haight-Ashbury, and climaxed with San Francisco's ascension to LSD capital of the world. The new approval of sensualities had caught up with my long-cherished desire to celebrate the flexible beauties of the body unclothed. How could I express this on film?

Recently I had become obsessed by beds, by the bed as humanity's most enjoyable article of furniture. I had written "a play in four bedrooms" called *Bedlam:* four undressed dramas occurring concurrently in four Modesto locations. I had even proposed a revue called *Beds* to Herbert Blau at his Actors' Workshop. Neither of these projects had reached production stage. Therefore in considering a film to delight a discerning sybarite like Ledoux, I devised scenes for a romp of the human comedy enacted on a bed in an open-air Eden. The argument of my vision was simple enough: "All the world's a bed, and men and women merely dreamers."

To begin, I needed a bed and a place to photograph it. An antique shop in Sausalito let me "borrow" a sturdy white wrought iron double bed. (When I "returned" it months later, the bed had been reduced to a bundle of chipped metal parts held together by ropes.) As a location site for an undressed caper what could be more congenial than Druid Heights? It had the advantage of remoteness and a mountain meadow to work in. The remoteness became a disadvantage only when a prop, a tool, or an absent performer had to be fetched. Roger Somers played his saxophone as a naked Pan, Alan Watts portrayed a doctor of both medicine and divinity, Elsa declined to be involved in any way. I needed many examples of Adam's descendants to populate my intimate vaudeville of desire. I enticed old friends to participate: Imogen Cunningham, Jean Varda, Kermit, Gavin Arthur, and famous model Florence Allen, as well as members of Anna Halprin's dance company. Desloge provided young beauties and hippie pals.

In that season of "Make Love Not War" Druid Heights enjoyed a blithe summer. Picnics and pot kept the mood festive. Inventing escapades for the camera excited me. But *The Bed* almost didn't make it to Belgium in time. When it was finally edited I could not persuade any commercial laboratory to print it. From Eastman in Rochester to Consolidated in Los Angeles I received curt refusals: it was against official policy to print "frontal nudity." Finally I located an illegal pornography outfit which printed much frontal nudity between midnight and dawn in the rear of a building on a back street in East Palo Alto.

To my astonishment *The Bed* won many prizes at world festivals. Furthermore it broke a taboo: frontal nudity soon populated all avant-garde screens. Only two years later my subsequent project, totally nude *Golden Positions*, encountered no difficulty with any printer. To my further astonishment, *The Bed* came into widespread use as a relaxing introduction to consciousness-raising seminars and training programs for social, hospital, and psychiatric workers. When I was about to undergo a colonoscopy at the Marin General Hospital, the attendant nurse saw my name on the chart and cried out "Doctor, did you ever see *The Bed*? It's the most wonderful crazy movie you could ever imagine," babbling on until the doctor barked, "Nurse, let's pay attention to our work. Please anesthetize the patient in the right buttock."

With notoriety I was better able to garner support for film projects and was offered additional teaching at the San Francisco Art Institute. Also I was asked to serve on the selection committee of Anthology Film Archives with Jonas Mekas, P. Adams Sitney, and Peter Kubelka. Jerome Hill financed my acquisition of an editing studio and the equipment for it, as well as making possible *The Golden Positions*. Other friends aided later works. I owe to Pauline Kael my grants from the Guggenheim Foundation and to Sally Dixon of the Carnegie Institute my NEA awards. With these I rolled into a momentum of activity, producing a film a year from 1968 to 1974.

After honoring the Dance of Life in *The Bed* I paid tribute to the Human Body (in *The Golden Positions*), to the Eternal Child (in

This is It), to the Eternal Return (in *The Water Circle*), to the Eternal Moment (in *High Kukus*), and most ambitiously to the Eternal Feminine (in *Dreamwood*). These eternalities praised the beauty of humans, the surprises of soul, and the necessity of merriment.

I cherish my collaborators in the Brotherhood of Light during the sixties and seventies: Fred Padula, Ed Jenkins, David Myers, and even crotchety John Schofill whose perfectionism illuminated the puzzles I dealt with in *Dreamwood*. In this complex work — my *Blood of a Poet*, P. Adams Sitney called it — I tried to come to terms with the powers of the Feminine that had wounded my early life. Envisioning a hero quest into the labyrinth of a Perilous Forest like Goethe's "Realm of the Mothers" I had my protagonist confront avatars of the Goddess — minx, virgin, amazon, muse, hag, — until by crawling into the womb of Death to be reborn, he is able to unite his seed with the earth and heal the war of opposites within himself.

In *Dreamwood* I did take some revenge on my hermaphroditic mother. I had my hero smash with an axe the mirror of a dressing table at which bearded Roger Somers sat primping, attired in the gown worn by the goddess of Death. *Dreamwood* too was filmed in and around Druid Heights when Margo St. James lived there while organizing the prostitutes of San Francisco into a union. Versatile Margo enacted most of the goddesses in the film.

When on my sixtieth birthday in 1973 I was honored with retrospective exhibits in London and in New York, I felt it was time to fold up my career as a filmmaker. I had produced seven films in ten years. I thought I had said everything I had to say, except perhaps for some graceful farewell. Besides, my sagging energies were reflected in my home life. In the marriage bed I had encountered the consternation of impotence. Suzanna's resentment of this took an inevitable turn: she asked me to move out of our bedroom and sleep in my studio.

Urologists wanted to operate on me but Jerome Hill, who suffered from prostate cancer, sent me to a doctor who injected me in the ass with an extract of bull's balls. The only result from this cure: difficulty in sitting down. Of course the problem was as much psychological as physical. The babies were now in public school, Suzanna was trying to make a go of an ethnic gift shop, and I couldn't help being more interested in my collaborations and my poetry than in husbandry and parenting. To try bridging the breach we consulted a marriage counselor. After we had each unburdened our grievances it was plain that the relationship could never recover the joviality it once enjoyed.

In 1972 the City of Modesto invited me to inaugurate a new county library with a suitable speech since I was the only writer they could find who had been born in the town. When my class in film directing at San Francisco State learned of the prospect they insisted on giving me a hero's return by carrying me on a litter through the town at the head of a costumed parade. This actually took place at high noon on the Friday of my scheduled evening speech. They dressed me in a hand-painted magician's cloak and a pheasant-feathered hat. Masked and bedecked, they danced whirlingly behind me as I was carried down the main street. The populace did not seem to appreciate the pearls I cast in front of them. A few looked disgusted, many mocked, others fled.

At my request our cortege progressed to the Oddfellows Cemetery where my ancestors lay buried. I had not visited it in many years. Among the inscriptions of names and dates I experienced a shudder of mortality and a rush of nostalgia. I thought of my grandmother's milky bosom, my mother's brown nipple, my grandfather's long bulge in his trousers, my Aunt Esto's painful limp, my father's strong arms, my Uncle Jim's lap, Dr. Robertson's warm hands, my starry angel's wand. . . .

For the Modesto events I had asked my favorite student, Ed Jenkins, to film everything in slow motion to differentiate it from a newsreel look. When I studied this footage it triggered the possibility of an autobiographical film bearing witness to the progressions of my life. Was there any meaning to my devious pilgrim's progress? However much of Jung and Watts I may have absorbed, the more I thought I knew, the less I understood. But I could pay tribute to my ups and downs by quoting from earlier films and imagining new sequences like my mythic second birth from a naked Hermes and a nightgowned Aphrodite. I could also persuade my son Orion to enact my childhood puzzlements. In the end, though only twenty minutes long, *Testament* offered a collage of my creative efforts and a reflection upon the mysteries of cinema and life.

I owe the lively texture of *Testament* to Jenkins, an ingratiating and resourceful redhead who had hunted in Kenya and fished off the Great Barrier Reef. His devoted companionship on many a location shooting provided a cheerful antidote to the anxieties of the home place.

Although I had intended *Testament* as an epitaph I had some unfinished cinema business in Pittsburgh. Robert Haller of Pittsburgh Filmmakers had been raising money to help me fulfill a long held ambition: a closeup exploration of bodily geography. I saw this as an intimate companion piece to the full-length nudity in *The Golden Positions*. Taking a leave of absence from the San Francisco Art Institute to collaborate with Robert Gaylor's camera, I explored textures and crevices of Pennsylvania flesh. This foray into erogenous zones acquired an inevitable title: *Erogeny*.

When I brought home the unedited reels of Pittsburgh intimacies, one of my graduate students requested a private interview to show me a project he had completed in my absence. It was titled *Perisphere* and carried a dedication to me. I had not expected to be bowled over by a masterly tour de force. Its subject was nothing less than the circulation of all things as symbolized by a rhythmic sweep of back and forth arcs filmed from the center of a traffic circle in Berkeley. Its cars went round with its houses and its houses went round with the world. The creator of this remarkable work was a native of Canada named Joel Singer. I praised him with an embrace.

I was not prepared for what embraced me in return. He had set me on fire.

Who was he? Who was this ardent young man with cascading curls and sharp profile? Why did my soul explode into rocket fire when he touched me? Was he a Promethean demigod masquerading as a student? Why did cherubim clap their wings around us? I consulted available oracles: astrologer, psychic, swami, palmist. All assured me: This is It! This is soul mate stuff. This is your Big It!

Had an aging songbird from Modesto met his match in a young jock from Montreal? Joel was twenty-six and I was sixty-one. This discrepancy made no difference to him, while I of course relished it. He seemed to embody the complete comrade lover I had never expected to encounter in the flesh. Besides, he looked exactly as I had always imagined Jesus.

Joel brought me true "psychic wholeness" by giving me the missing reality of myself. At last I could become fully my own kind of man, giving in as well as cutting loose. Reinvigorated I was ready to begin life anew. Together we made books of poetry. Together we made eight films beginning with *Together* in 1976. The last of these collaborations in 1988 was *Scattered Remains*, the poet of me as seen by Joel.

My children delighted in Joel's willingness to be a second father to them. Unfortunately Suzanna could not also accept him as a new member of the family. Though the divorce was not amicable, in our lively laughing years she and I had enjoyed much that I am grateful to remember.

In Montreal on Christmas Eve of 1976 Joel Singer and I were secretly married in a storefront chapel on Boulevard St. Laurent by a Marist priest named Father Rainer. The witness was an asthmatic acolyte. No make-believe propped up this wedding: it glowed with the radiance of miracle.

That snowy evening after a fine French dinner we attended midnight mass in the Cathedral of Notre Dame. During the "Gloria" I saw above the altar my beloved Hermy wafting in spirals, smiling and waving his sparkler. Mighty spry for an angel in his sixties. Waving back, I chanted my favorite mantra, "Praise and thanks. Praise and thanks."

An excerpt from my poem *Wondrous the Merge* reveals the heart of our story:

He said I held the key to his existence
He said he knew when he first saw me
that I was the reason for his birth
He claimed that important deities
had opened his head three times
to place my star in his brow

This is preposterous   I said
I have a wife in the suburbs
I have mortgages   children   in-laws
and a position in the community
I thoroughly sympathize   said He
Why else have I come to your rescue? . . .

At Beck's Motel on the 7th of April
we went to bed for three days
disheveled the king size sheets
never changed the Do Not Disturb
ate only the fruits of discovery
drank semen and laughter and sweat

He seasoned my mouth
  sweetened my neck
  coddled my nipple
  nuzzled my belly
  groomed my groin
  buffed my buttock
  garnished my pubis

renovated my phallus
remodeled my torso
until I cried out
until I cried
    I am Yes
    I am your Yes
        I am I am your
            Yes Yes Yes. . . .

I severed my respectabilities
and bought a yellow mobile home
in an unlikely neighborhood
He moved in his toaster   his camera
and his eagerness to become
my courier seed-carrier and consort

Above all he brought the flying carpet
that upholsters his boundless embrace
Year after year he takes me soaring
out to the ecstasies of the cosmos
that await all beings in love

One day we shall not bother to return

BOOKS BY JAMES BROUGHTON

FILMS BY JAMES BROUGHTON

1988	Scattered Remains
1983	Devotions
1981	The Gardener of Eden
1979	Hermes Bird
1977	Song of the Godbody
1976	Together
1976	Erogeny
1974	Testament
1972	Dreamwood
1971	This is It
1970	The Golden Positions
1969	Nuptiae
1968	The Bed
1953	The Pleasure Garden
1951	Loony Tom
1951	Four in the Afternoon
1950	Adventures of Jimmy
1948	Mother's Day
1946	The Potted Psalm

These films are available on 16mm from
Canyon Cinema, 2325 Third St. San Francisco CA 94107
and on video cassette from Facets,
1517 West Fullerton Ave. Chicago IL 60614

CITY LIGHTS PUBLICATIONS

Acosta, Juvenal, ed. LIGHT FROM A NEARBY WINDOW
Allen, Roberta. AMAZON DREAM
Angulo de, Jaime. INDIANS IN OVERALLS
Angulo de, G. & J. JAIME IN TAOS
Artaud, Antonin. ARTAUD ANTHOLOGY
Bataille, Georges. EROTISM: Death and Sensuality
Bataille, Georges. THE IMPOSSIBLE
Bataille, Georges. STORY OF THE EYE
Bataille, Georges. THE TEARS OF EROS
Baudelaire, Charles. INTIMATE JOURNALS
Baudelaire, Charles. TWENTY PROSE POEMS
Bowles, Paul. A HUNDRED CAMELS IN THE COURTYARD
Broughton, James. COMING UNBUTTONED
Broughton, James. MAKING LIGHT OF IT
Brown, Rebecca. ANNIE OAKLEY'S GIRL
Brown, Rebecca. THE TERRIBLE GIRLS
Bukowski, Charles. THE MOST BEAUTIFUL WOMAN IN TOWN
Bukowski, Charles. NOTES OF A DIRTY OLD MAN
Bukowski, Charles. TALES OF ORDINARY MADNESS
Burroughs, William S. THE BURROUGHS FILE
Burroughs, William S. THE YAGE LETTERS
Cassady, Neal. THE FIRST THIRD
Choukri, Mohamed. FOR BREAD ALONE
CITY LIGHTS REVIEW #2: AIDS & the Arts
CITY LIGHTS REVIEW #3: Media and Propaganda
CITY LIGHTS REVIEW #4: Literature / Politics / Ecology
Cocteau, Jean. THE WHITE BOOK (LE LIVRE BLANC)
Codrescu, Andrei, ed. EXQUISITE CORPSE READER
Cornford, Adam. ANIMATIONS
Corso, Gregory. GASOLINE
Daumal, René. THE POWERS OF THE WORD
David-Neel, Alexandra. SECRET ORAL TEACHINGS IN TIBETAN
        BUDDHIST SECTS
Deleuze, Gilles. SPINOZA: Practical Philosophy
Dick, Leslie. KICKING
Dick, Leslie. WITHOUT FALLING
di Prima, Diane. PIECES OF A SONG: Selected Poems
Doolittle, Hilda (H.D.) NOTES ON THOUGHT & VISION
Ducornet, Rikki. ENTERING FIRE
Duras, Marguerite. DURAS BY DURAS
Eidus, Janice. VITO LOVES GERALDINE
Eberhardt, Isabelle. THE OBLIVION SEEKERS
Fenollosa, Ernest. CHINESE WRITTEN CHARACTER AS A MEDIUM
        FOR POETRY
Ferlinghetti, Lawrence. PICTURES OF THE GONE WORLD

Ferlinghetti, Lawrence. SEVEN DAYS IN NICARAGUA LIBRE
Finley, Karen. SHOCK TREATMENT
Ford, Charles Henri. OUT OF THE LABYRINTH: Selected Poems
Franzen, Cola, transl. POEMS OF ARAB ANDALUSIA
García Lorca, Federico. BARBAROUS NIGHTS: Legends & Plays
García Lorca, Federico. ODE TO WALT WHITMAN & OTHER POEMS
García Lorca, Federico. POEM OF THE DEEP SONG
Gil de Biedma, Jaime. LONGING: SELECTED POEMS
Ginsberg, Allen. HOWL & OTHER POEMS
Ginsberg, Allen. KADDISH & OTHER POEMS
Ginsberg, Allen. REALITY SANDWICHES
Ginsberg, Allen. PLANET NEWS
Ginsberg, Allen. THE FALL OF AMERICA
Ginsberg, Allen. MIND BREATHS
Ginsberg, Allen. PLUTONIAN ODE
Goethe, J. W. von. TALES FOR TRANSFORMATION
Hayton-Keeva, Sally, ed. VALIANT WOMEN IN WAR AND EXILE
Herron, Don. THE DASHIELL HAMMETT TOUR: A Guidebook
Herron, Don. THE LITERARY WORLD OF SAN FRANCISCO
Higman, Perry, tr. LOVE POEMS FROM SPAIN AND SPANISH AMERICA
Jaffe, Harold. EROS: ANTI-EROS
Jenkins, Edith. AGAINST A FIELD SINISTER
Kerouac, Jack. BOOK OF DREAMS
Kerouac, Jack. POMES ALL SIZES
Kerouac, Jack. SCATTERED POEMS
Lacarrière, Jacques. THE GNOSTICS
La Duke, Betty. COMPANERAS
La Loca. ADVENTURES ON THE ISLE OF ADOLESCENCE
Lamantia, Philip. MEADOWLARK WEST
Laughlin, James. SELECTED POEMS: 1935-1985
Le Brun, Annie. SADE: On the Brink of the Abyss
Lowry, Malcolm. SELECTED POEMS
Mackey, Nathaniel. SCHOOL OF UDHRA
Marcelin, Philippe-Thoby. THE BEAST OF THE HAITIAN HILLS
Masereel, Frans. PASSIONATE JOURNEY
Mayakovsky, Vladimir. LISTEN! EARLY POEMS
Mrabet, Mohammed. THE BOY WHO SET THE FIRE
Mrabet, Mohammed. THE LEMON
Mrabet, Mohammed. LOVE WITH A FEW HAIRS
Mrabet, Mohammed. M'HASHISH
Murguía, A. & B. Paschke, eds. VOLCAN: Poems from Central America
Murillo, Rosario. ANGEL IN THE DELUGE
Paschke, B. & D. Volpendesta, eds. CLAMOR OF INNOCENCE
Pasolini, Pier Paolo. ROMAN POEMS
Pessoa, Fernando. ALWAYS ASTONISHED
Peters, Nancy J., ed. WAR AFTER WAR (City Lights Review #5)
Poe, Edgar Allan. THE UNKNOWN POE